The Profits of Extermination

How U.S. Corporate Power
is Destroying Colombia

Francisco Ramírez Cuellar

Introduction and Translation
Aviva Chomsky

Common Courage Press   Monroe, Maine

ISBN 1-56751-322-0 paper ISBN 1-56751-323-9 hard back
ISBN-13: 9781567513226 paper;
ISBN-13: 9781567513233 hard back
Sintraminercol
Office of the President and
Human Rights Investigation Team
SINTRAMINERCOL

Union of Workers in the National Mining Company Minercol,
Ltda.

Affiliate of Funtraenergética (Federation of Mining and
Energy Workers) and the CUT (Colombian Unified Workers
Central)

Sintraminercol
Calle 32 #13-07
Bogotá, Colombia
57-1-2456581/ 57-1-5612829   sintrami@telecom.com.co

Library of Congress Cataloging-in-Publication Data is
available on request from the publisher

Common Courage Press
121 Red Barn Road
Monroe, ME 04951
800-497-3207 fax (207) 525-3068
info@commoncouragepress.com
Printed in Canada   First Printing

The publication original Spanish edition of this book was
made possible through the support of the Northern Ireland Public
Service Association (NIPSA) and Justice for Colombia.

To Alessandro Baratta, my teacher.

My brother, who was at our side in the struggle.

Contents

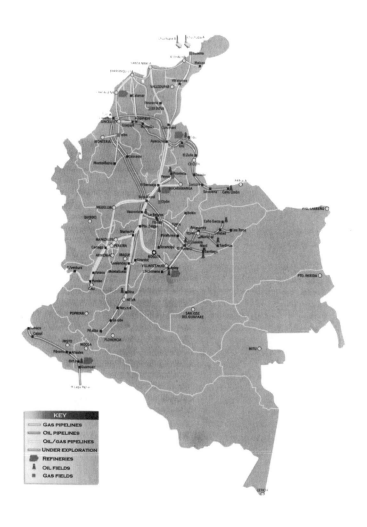

Map 1. Oil and gas deposits and pipelines.

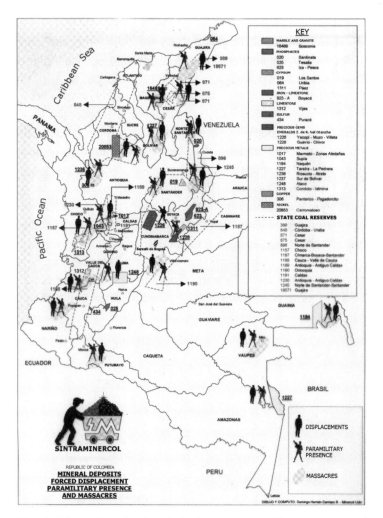

Map 2. Mineral deposits, forced displacement, paramilitary presence and massacres.

Acknowledgements

Sintraminercol is grateful to the following for their invaluable support for this project: The Human Rights organization Minga, with whom we began to work on this project six years ago; the Cinep (Centro de Investigación y Educación Popular) and Justicia y Paz database; the CUT Human Rights Department; the Nomadesc Association, with whom we collaborated in the final phase of this project; Amnesty International; the Canadian Auto Workers union (CAW); Kathy Price and Bill Fairbairn; the miners, peasants, men, women and children who have been the victims of this war of extermination; Cuco and Gildardo, who we will remember forever; the independent researchers, journalists, and everyone who in one way or another contributed to our work and made it possible for the world to learn about the Colombian situation. To all of these people and organizations, our heartfelt thanks.

Translator's Acknowledgements

I can't even begin to list everybody whose work with the North Shore Colombia Solidarity Committee has led up to the English translation of this book. We have also been lucky to be able to collaborate with other wonderful organizations: Sintraminercol, Yanama, and Minga (in Colombia), Mines and Communities and the Colombia Solidarity Campaign (in London), Kairos (in Canada), the International Labor Rights Fund, PressurePoint, Colombia Vive, the Committee for Social Justice in Colombia, and Witness for Peace (in the United States). Several photographers generously allowed us to include their work. Special thanks for help with the translation to Janie Simmons, Andy Klatt, Richard Solly, and, of course, Francisco.

Translator's note

In translating this book, I have made some adjustments to make it more accessible to an English-speaking audience. I have added or expanded several footnotes to explain mining and legal terminology that I assume is not general knowledge. I have also tried to add English-language sources, where available, to further document information where the original references only Spanish sources.

Introduction to the English Edition

Aviva Chomsky

T hree things happened in the spring of 2002 that changed my life dramatically. First, I received an email message from a stranger, Alan Hanscom. A local environmental organization had just learned that the Salem Harbor Power Station burns coal from Colombia, he said. Did I know anything about coal mining in Colombia? "How silly," I thought, "Just because I teach Latin American history, people think I know about EVERYTHING that happens in Latin America." I didn't even bother to answer the message.

Then a student told me that he had seen an impressive slide presentation on Colombia, at a library in Boston, and wanted to invite the speaker to Salem State. This time I was a bit more receptive; I'm always looking for an opportunity to organize political events on campus. A lot of people turned out for the event, including the mystery emailer, Alan. This time I was a little more intrigued when he introduced himself to me. "I'll see what I can find out," I promised rashly.

Finally, that spring I was teaching a course on Central American history. When we discussed the dramatic and horrifying events in Guatemala in the 1980s, as always, students repeatedly asked me "how could all these things have been going on, and we didn't even know about it?" My answer came easily: "What's even worse, " I told them, "is that these things are going on NOW in Colombia, and nobody knows about it." The so-called "drug war" in Colombia, I told them, served the purpose that "communism" served for the U.S. government in Central America in the 1980s. The root of the problem was social injustice and foreign intervention to secure profits by

Bulldozers preparing the ground for the Cerrejón Zona Norte Mine, 1983.
Photograph by Deborah Pacini Hernandez.

preserving social inequality; drugs, like communism, were merely a pretext for intervention.

After making that statement several times, I realized it was actually time for me to find out more about Colombia. I began with the coal that was coming into Salem regularly, transported in huge ships into Salem Harbor in 40,000 metric tonne loads. The coal, I discovered, came from the Cerrejón Zona Norte mine in Colombia's Guajira peninsula, owned and operated jointly by the Exxon corporation and the Colombian government. I learned that my friend and colleague Deborah Pacini had spent the summer of 1983 in the Guajira researching the impact of the mine—which was then in the beginnings of the construction phase—on the Wayuu indigenous people in the Guajira. Although many Wayuu were hopeful that the mine would bring jobs and development to their region, they were also wary about the impact this huge operation would have on

Trailer camp for temporary workers brought in during the construction phase at the Cerrejón Zona Norte Mine, 1983. Photograph by Deborah Pacini Hernandez.

their traditional lifestyles.

Foreign corporations and foreign governments funded this project from the start. In February 1982, the U.S. Export-Import Bank approved a $12.3 million loan to a Spanish company to purchase U.S. earth-moving equipment for Colombian mining; Canada's Export Development Bank followed with a $160 million line of credit to Colombia to purchase Canadian equipment, and the Export-Import Bank countered with another $375 million in August.[1] In the end the Export-Import Bank lent $1.5 billion to the Colombian government, paying for its entire share in the project.[2]

Pacini studied the site for eight weeks in 1983 and described it in detail: "The road has been completed since 1981, and the construction of the port, warehouses, workers' camps, hospital, water treatment facilities, etc., is considerably

Typical Wayuu dwelling for temporary use during migration. Note the cooking pots hanging outside. The woman wears the traditional "manta" or long flowing brightly-colored dress. Photograph by Deborah Pacini Hernandez.

advanced. Less construction is visible at the mine area, where the task of clearing the land of vegetation for the mine and mine infrastructure is immense—much greater than that required for the port. Temporary workers' camps have been erected and more are being built to accommodate the projected peak work force during the construction phase of about 7,000 (although more recent estimates place the eventual construction work force at 10,000). Once production begins in 1985-1986, the permanent work force of about 3,000 workers will be housed in several towns located along the southern part of the mine-port road. The infrastructures of these towns will be expanded to accommodate the influx of workers."[3]

The pastoral nomadic Wayuu lacked legal title to their ancestral lands; thus when the potential for profit arose in those lands, the government declared them to be "baldíos" or untitled land, and granted the mine, in 1981, 29,000 hectares in four "reservas" (areas claimed by the government for economic development purposes) for the railroad, road, port, and for construction materials. Some 200 Wayuu families were offered compensation for their confiscated ranchos. As Pacini notes, however, the compensation was minimal (much smaller than that offered to displaced residents in the southern part of the peninsula), and it was culturally inappropriate because the lands taken were in fact part of a much larger system of migration and kinship, not just the location of specific residences.[4]

Along the northern coast, Wayuu fishing in the Bahía de Portete was halted as the harbor was dredged and turned over to the shipping of coal. Media Luna, a Wayuu community of approximately 750 on the southern end of the bay, was the first permanent community to be displaced by the mine. After negotiations with Exxon in 1982 (punctuated by "angry discussions and physical threats") residents agreed to move their homes, their farms and their cemetery to a nearby location in order to allow for the construction of the port. When the company demanded that they move again a few years later, seven families (42 people) refused, despite continuing problems they faced with pollution caused by the construction. The company walled off the area and surrounded it with armed guards. Despite constant harassment, including lack of water, refusal of building permits, and blacklisting of community members from employment, residents remained there, living in conditions described in 2001 as "like a Nazi concentration camp."[5]

In 1982 a group of Wayuu formed Yanama—a Wayuu word meaning "collective work"—an organization to defend

An early meeting of the Wayuu organization Yanama, 1983. Photograph by Deborah Pacini Hernandez.

their rights in the face of the incursions on their lands. Yanama was successful in preventing the company from leveling the sacred Cerro de la Teta mountain, though it remains inside the company's "reserva." Some Wayuu also tried—mostly unsuccessfully—to appeal to government agencies charged with the defense of indigenous rights. The major strategy, according to Pacini, was "invasión" or the establishment of residences directly along the railroad strip designed to establish a presence and prevent construction. In the summer of 1983, over 1000 ranchos had been built, effectively halting railroad construction.[6] Yanama also worked to have their lands declared a "resguardo" (what in English would be a reservation; granting title to the indigenous community as a whole).[7]

In 1996, a Wayuu representative described the impact of the mine on his people at a meeting in Wisconsin: "The

Yanama organizer Remedios Fajardo, 1983. Photograph by Deborah Pacini Hernandez.

construction of the mine had a devastating effect on the lives of approximately 90 Wayuu apushis (matrilineal kinship groupings) who saw their houses, corrals, cleared ground and cemeteries flattened for the construction of a road from El Cerrejón to the new port of Puerto Bolívar, with no respect for indigenous rights. The excavation of the open pit has also caused the adjoining rivers and streams to dry up, along with people's drinking wells."[8]

A 2001 report documented the depressingly predictable long-term effect of the mine on the indigenous Wayuu communities: the proliferation of alcoholism and prostitution, the loss of sacred spaces, a rise in death rates due to poisoning and contamination from the mine and its wastes, loss of cultural integrity and identity, and increasing poverty.[9] The mine's encroachment on indigenous lands has continued unabated over the last 25 years.

Some of these violations were summed up at an international meeting held in London in 2001. The final declaration of the meeting read, in part: "We have seen our peoples suffering for many years from mining in all stages and forms, and from exploration to development through to abandonment. Industrial mining has caused grievous pain and irreparable destruction to our culture, our identities and our very lives. Our traditional lands have been taken, and the wealth seized, without our consent or benefit. Invariably, mining imposed upon our communities has poisoned our waters, destroyed our livelihoods and our food sources, disrupted our social relationships, and created sickness and injury in our families. Often our communities have been divided by 'imported' civil conflicts. Increasing mechanization has denied many of us the role we once had as mineworkers."[10]

Having learned about the origins of our coal, a group of local residents here on Boston's North Shore began to work with a Seattle-based organization, PressurePoint, to bring Wayuu indigenous leader and Yanama founder Remedios Fajardo to the United States to address the Exxon shareholders meeting in Dallas in May of 2002. When Remedios and her partner, Armando Pérez Araujo, a lawyer representing indigenous and

Afro-Colombian villagers in front of their former homes, bulldozed by Exxon to make room for mine expansion. Tabaco, La Guajira, August 2001. From "The Destruction of Tabaco" produced by PressurePoint

Villagers from Tabaco. From "The Destruction of Tabaco" produced by PressurePoint.

Villagers from Tabaco. From "The Destruction of Tabaco" produced by PressurePoint.

Afro-Colombian communities displaced by the mine, came to Salem, they met with the mayor, the city council, and different community groups. "We've been struggling for 20 years to get the story out about what the mine is doing to our people," Remedios told me. "No one has ever wanted to listen to us before."

Most of the audiences Armando and Remedios addressed in and around Salem did want to listen. The Salem City Council passed a resolution asking Exxon to relocate villagers who had been displaced; community groups offered to organize material aid and to try to draw public attention to the people who were the victims. There were some, however, who declined to meet with them: in particular, the management of the power plant and the union there.

We explained to Armando and Remedios that both the

Remedios Fajardo, Armondo Pérez, and local environmentalist Lynn Nadeau in front of the Salem Harbor Power Station, May 2002. Photograph by Aviva Chomsky.

union and the management at the plant were very worried about any negative publicity that could affect the plant. We were especially concerned about our inability to make links with the union. Workers at the plant seemed to fear that any discussion that might reflect badly on the plant could threaten their jobs. Yet we also knew that some sectors of the U.S. labor movement had taken a strong stand for human and labor rights in Colombia.

"You should invite Francisco Ramírez to meet with you," Armando and Remedios agreed. "He is the president of Sintraminercol (Sindicato de Trabajadores de la Empresa Nacional Minera), the mineworkers union in Colombia, and his union has faced all of these issues. He really understands how workers' rights are linked to human rights, to everybody's human rights; how you can try to protect coal miners' jobs at the same time that you work to protect the rights of communities affected by the mines. His union sees the mining sector as a whole, and is working for the rights of EVERYBODY affected by the sector. Our interests are not in conflict with those of the workers; we are not against the existence of the mine. We just want it to respect our rights."

We did invite Francisco, and in the fall of 2002 he spent a month based in Salem, also traveling for events in New York and Montreal. This time we were able to tour the plant and meet with both the union and the management, as well as with many other labor, school, academic, and community and political organizations. Audiences were unfailingly impressed with Francisco's compelling narrative about how Colombia's mineral and energy resources were a key to understanding the violence there, his evidence of U.S. government and corporate complicity in crimes against humanity in Colombia, and his vision for a more humane world. He had already survived four attempts against his life by Colombian paramilitary groups that wanted to silence his message.

Although we were awed by the facts and figures Francisco presented showing the links between Colombia's mineral wealth, foreign investment, and violence and human rights

Francisco Ramírez (second from right) meeting with union leaders
and plant manager at the Salem Harbor Power Station, October 2002.
Photograph by Claudia Chuber.

violations, we were also frustrated because we only had his
powerful words, with no documentation to back them up. We
wanted to continue to spread his message, but none of us had
his grasp of the details. "We'll publish all of this information
soon," he promised us.

Finally we have in our hands the document, the result of
many years of research by Sintraminercol, showing how the
Colombian people have been the victim of foreign companies,
governments, and institutions that want to take advantage of
the country's mineral and energy resources. As always, I am
humbled by the struggles of the people in countries that have
been the victims of our affluence here in the United States, by
their commitment to creating a more just world, and by the

risks they face in working and organizing to achieve that goal. I am proud and grateful that I can be part of bringing this story to a broader English-speaking public.

Salem, Massachusetts
May 2004

Prologue to the Spanish Edition

Javier Giraldo, MSJ

One of the most heart-wrenching episodes in Colombia's recent history—for those of us who still retain some human sensibility in this maelstrom of violence—occurred on the night of April 25, 1997 in the town of Río Viejo in Bolívar Department. A large paramilitary force took over the town at 7:30 pm. They dragged many of the residents violently from their homes, forced them to lie down in the main street, shirtless, and whipped them. When they identified Juan Camacho Herrera, a member of the Agro-Mining Association of the South of Bolívar—a grassroots organization that represents poor miners who engage in small-scale artisanal mining, sifting small grains of gold from the earth to survive—they assassinated him with seven gunshots. They then beheaded him with a machete. They carried his head through the town and kicked it around. Finally they nailed it to a post with his face looking towards the Serranía de San Lucas, warning the stupefied residents that they were planning on taking control of this mining zone.

Our vision is often limited by ideological conditionings that prevent us from capturing the real dimensions of a horrific event like this one.

The most scrupulous jurists, versed in international law, might suggest that we focus on the delinquent conduct of the lawbreakers who committed the crime, taking care not to contaminate our analysis with a political or ideological slant that would adulterate the purity of the Law. According to them, we must isolate the crimes of homicide and torture from the context of the social struggle of the victims, from the problem of natural resources and their legislation, and from the problem of land ownership and the unequal distribution of wealth. In addition, these jurists might tell us that under no circumstances can we acknowledge a crime like this as part of a pattern, even if it is shown that since 1995 occurrences like this one have become routine in the region. And we certainly cannot investigate this type of crime as an expression of an official policy, even if it can be shown that actions by the public security forces are coordinated in the length and breadth of the country with the actions of the paramilitaries, following a logic of persecuting organizations that don't share official policies. A juridical approach conditioned in this way limits its focus to the tree's final fruit, studiously ignoring the tree's leaves and its branches, its trunk, its roots, and its sap—precisely what others might consider crucial to understanding and characterizing a sickness in the fruit.

In a similar vein, a bishop concerned with finding a solution to the conflict that engulfs us might even forbid the preservation of Juan Camacho's memory on the wall of one of the churches in his diocese. Recently, one bishop actually ordered that the names of the victims engraved on the wall of the humble chapel in a village be erased, alleging that this memory was harmful because it focused attention on the past and kept the wounds and the hatreds open. We must forget, then, according to him, and turn our faces from the victims of the past, in order to get beyond the violence. According to his theology, this is called "forgiveness" or "reconciliation."

If we were to adhere to the perspective that has acquired currency in the reigning spheres of power, the memory of Juan Camacho would have to be definitively buried if we hope to some day achieve peace. This government's High Commissioner for Peace, the psychiatrist Luis Carlos Restrepo, wrote an article in 1997 that perhaps caught the attention of the future President of the Republic and moved him to offer Restrepo the position. Referring to the need to bury the memory of the popular leader Jorge Eliécer Gaitán, Restrepo stated, "When a culture begins to turn into a field of unburied corpses—that stalk us with their stench so that we will spill blood again and satiate their lust for vengeance—it becomes urgent for us to take up the profession of grave-diggers. What we need are astute teachers of forgetting who help us to recover our strength and our innocence in such moments when the cult of the dead—and the powers that represent them—start to asphyxiate the living. The time has come to sign a new pact with those who are gone, writing their names on comets sending them off on the wind. The time has come to end our solidarity with history, to abandon our loyalty to the homeland, if our homeland continues to be reduced to the collective stupidity of crushing life so that the blood of martyrs and *caudillos* remains alive."[1]

Shortly after Dr. Restrepo published this article, a paramilitary group under the name "Network for Citizens' Defense—Local Democracy" tried to force Jorge Eliécer's daughter Gloria Gaitán, under threat, to give up her position as director of the Gaitán Museum. They bolstered their demand by referring to Restrepo's article, stating "Dr. Restrepo, who provides our ideological orientation, says" and continuing, "it is true that Gaitán was poorly buried. We are going to bury him. We are going to accept the position of grave-diggers so that Colombia forgets him once and for all, to end the hatred that his name inflames. That is why we are determined to eliminate this stubborn obstacle that his daughter presents, and demand that she step down from her post. If Gloria Gaitán does not step down before next July 26, which is the date that we gave her to retire from this trench of subversion represented by her father's house, we vow to dynamite the Museum and her father's tomb, and to make her and her family reunite with Gaitán so that we can finally bury them well and deeply, so that they do not continue to feed with their memory the flame of hatred of their followers who drink their blood and consume their ideas of retaliation and death…"

Discourses are often based on deeply incoherent ideas and contradictions hidden under layers of rhetoric. Hatred is condemned by those who inspire hatred. Rights are defended by those who crush rights, under the pretext of respecting the purity of the law. Memory is forbidden in the name of a different memory that is being created. Justice is even administered by those who forbid people to look at injustices. And our beliefs have to adjust to the incoherencies, or else they have to be diverted and hushed, if we don't want to be seen as anachronistic or accused of crimes "against the dominant society." This society is prepared to integrate us if we accept its dogmas or at least don't question them: law without ethics; forgiveness without truth or restitution; justice that accepts injustices; memory without a past; social solidarity that remains oblivious to inequality and violence.

In the face of these dogmas, this book that we present to the reader is "heretical." Sintraminercol writes with the authority of a union that knows the State's mining policies inside and out. It has tried to offer a vision of the tragic reality that envelopes us that is free of pressures and ideological conditioning. In doing so, it sheds light on the deep relations that exist between the most serious violations of human rights and the Colombian State's mining and energy policies.

From time immemorial, the Colombian State has attempted to base its economy on the most obsequious service to multinational capital. It has extended a hand to the instrument of paramilitarism in order to crush all social expressions whose economic logic is opposed to the interests of foreign capital. Similarly, it has made use of paramilitarism to destroy any political alternative that reclaims the visions and the rights of the most marginalized sectors of society. And in its zeal it has relativized and crushed all ethical values. It doesn't matter if peasants are massacred in huge numbers. It doesn't matter if we resort to the most chilling levels of savagery. It doesn't matter if communities are destroyed and hundreds of thousands of people are displaced. It doesn't matter if we steal and lie. It doesn't matter if we ally with drug traffickers, even under the hidden umbrella of the same entities who claim to be combating drug traffic at the international level, like the DEA. It doesn't matter if we steal helicopters from neighboring countries to supply clandestine centers of paramilitarism. It doesn't matter if we buy off or intimidate prosecutors, judges, or lawyers. It doesn't matter if we muzzle the press and pressure the churches to remain silent, to hide and to forget. Nothing matters as long as we protect the interests of large capital, whose altar is the only legitimate one in the unconfessed theology that inspires the real politics of a criminal State.

Bogotá, February 2004

Introduction

S intraminercol is a labor organization created in 1991 by the workers of what was then Mineralco S.A., the state mining company. Later, Mineralco combined with another state entity to form Minercol Ltda.

Our small union began by focusing on labor improvements, but later broadened its goals to fight against corruption, the greatest political ill in Colombia. This decision provoked the first death threats and the first attacks against its leaders. It also gave birth to a new type of activism, linking the union with the community. We began to expand our focus beyond labor rights, to take on the challenge of building a mining sector that would benefit our country's people as a whole. We would work from the perspective of the Colombian mineworker to develop a rational program for the mining sector that would also be technologically and environmentally sustainable.

In developing this program, we needed to research the different factors affecting mining in Colombia. We began in the zone where we were working, in the South of Bolívar region. We never imagined what we would discover while investigating the relations between the mining industry, the Colombian government, the Colombian military, the paramilitaries, the U.S. government, U.S. multinationals, the U.S. military, U.S. agencies, and the web that all of these have spun to "protect foreign investments." This book documents the results of our research over the past seven years.

The first section of this study will give a historical perspective of our situation.

Background

For centuries, the indigenous communities that occupied the territory that is today Colombia exploited its natural resources rationally, based on a cosmological vision of balance among man, nature, and the cosmos. This permitted very fragile environmental structures to remain unharmed. There were no natural disasters resulting from irrational exploitation of resources. Famines could be immediately controlled, and the food security of the people that inhabited the territory was not endangered. Minerals were only used for ceremonial purposes, for war and for traditional medicine.

With the arrival of the Spanish the situation changed dramatically, to the point where the very existence of the Amerindian population was threatened. The same happened to the African origin populations that were enslaved to replace the indigenous labor force being exterminated by the Spaniards. The insatiable ambition of the Spanish depleted the resources of the native indigenous communities, and of humanity.

The invaders did not discover new mineral deposits. Rather, they took advantage of those already known in regions like Marmato (in today's Caldas Department), the gold zones of Chocó and Cauca, as well as those in the Andean region in Antioquia, Tolima and Huila. The minerals they were most interested in were gold, silver, and some copper deposits used by the natives as a gold alloy.

The mining methods were primitive. The Spanish were forced to turn to the ancient knowledge of the indigenous communities, of the Africans and later, to somewhat more advanced techniques copied from the Germans. Beginning at the end of the eighteenth century, King Charles III brought

German engineers, who introduced new techniques that began to destroy fragile regional ecosystems in the areas that are today the Departments of Antioquia, Caldas, Cauca and Chocó, and in the region of Valle del Patía. The first mining legislation was the Rodas Decree of 1600 and the Mon y Velarde Decree of 1770. The entire production was destined for Spain and, through piracy, to England, allowing the development of industrial capitalism in European powers like Germany, France and England.

Later, after Colombia became independent in the early nineteenth century, mining operations passed into the hands of the state, which exploited them directly or transferred them to small and medium miners, who were concentrated in the central regions and in the rainforests of Chocó.[1] Part of the legislation was copied from the Spanish and French mining codes, which had always advocated state rights over natural resources, in contrast to the Anglo-Saxon tradition of private ownership.[2]

Simón Bolívar issued mining legislation in 1825, but it was not until 1886, when Rafael Núñez proclaimed the new Constitution, that Colombia had its first true Mining Code. It extended the Code of the sovereign state of Antioquia to the whole national territory. In the middle of the twentieth century the mining legislation was reformed once again.

Since the 1990s the World Bank has required the countries of Latin America to change their legislation to accommodate the needs of multinational companies, which have lobbied for the opening of markets to enable them to exploit the natural resources of our continent with no controls or restrictions. In the case of Colombia, several different actors have intervened: the international financial institutions—often the largest shareholders in the multinational companies—the governments of the countries where these multinationals are based, and the multinationals themselves. Their barefaced intervention in pursuit of their interests has led them to openly utilize all "legal" mechanisms to guarantee themselves colossal profits at the cost of the lives and the integrity of the Colombian people. During the last few decades and in the context of the imposition of the neoliberal economic model, they have manipulated bilateral and multilateral agreements in their own interest, they have acted as consultants in the drafting of new legislation, and, most seriously, they have participated openly in the Colombian state's military response against the strong popular resistance that has arisen among Colombians who oppose the process of globalization.

The popular organizations challenging the imposition of this model suffer from methods of state terrorism that include extermination, genocide, forced displacement, and every conceivable kind of violation of human rights, in the defense of the interests of the powerful and to protect foreign investment in Colombia.[3] These atrocities are being committed against a population that lacks the minimal resources for a decent life, and is suffering a civil war that has lasted for over fifty years and that has created—and continues to create—thousands of unnecessary victims.

A key statement by Bill Richardson (Secretary of Energy under Bill Clinton, 1998-2000) in Cartagena in 1999, sealed the fate of millions of Colombians: "The United States and its allies will invest millions of dollars in two areas of the Colombian economy, in the areas of mining and energy, and to secure these investments we are tripling military aid to Colombia."[4]

This aid to "secure investments" has produced 437 massacres in the mining zones in the past eight years, as well as over six thousand homicides in these regions. In addition, in the last ten years over two thousand unionists have been assassinated and hundreds illegally detained. Some three million Colombians have been displaced, and hundreds have been disappeared. Hundreds of popular organizations have been destroyed, and many indigenous and Afro-Colombian communities are in grave danger of extinction. Tax exemptions enjoyed by the multinationals have undermined Colombia's economy—causing losses of over thirteen billion dollars in just three huge coal and nickel mining projects. As a result 65% of Colombians live below the poverty line (earning under $3 a day), and 23.4 live in absolute poverty (earning under $2 a day). Up to 40% of Colombia's children do not attend school. Land and wealth are increasingly concentrated in the hands of a few.[5]

This study explains how governments and multinationals have manipulated international agreements, and how they have designed laws that serve their own interests. It details the military and paramilitary responses by the state and by these companies to "guarantee" investments. Finally, it shows the effects of these actions on the human rights of the Colombian people directly affected by mining-energy projects, and the disastrous impact of these projects on the country as a whole.

International Agreements

Agreements with international lending agencies

Multinationals and governments of several developed countries have been involved in shaping international lending agency policies. Their influence has led to policies that directly benefit multinationals individually or by sector. In some cases, in sectors like energy, petroleum, public services, health, mining, etc., multinationals have sought, and often obtained, benefits that favor the sector as a whole. In other cases, the multinational conglomerates' lawyers have drafted national legislation, and even obtained regulations that benefit particular companies in granting concessions for the exploitation of natural resources.

Nevertheless, one of the most lucrative changes has been the privatization of different sectors of production and services. For example, the energy generating sector was privatized and turned over to U.S. and Spanish companies, the health sector was taken over by multinationals like the Spanish Sanitas Internacional, and the petroleum sector by U.S., Canadian, English and recently, Spanish companies.[6]

Loan agreements Colombia has signed with the International Monetary Fund (IMF) and the World Bank (WB) ignore or pressure the legislative bodies. In some cases only the signature of the President of the Republic was required, making a mockery of or limiting constitutional control. These agreements contain public or, in some cases, secret or confidential clauses that limit or invalidate international treaties or agreements that Colombia has signed protecting biodiversity, imposing environmental restrictions on the exploitation of natural resources, controlling carbon emissions, or restricting areas of exploitation.

Other areas in which the IMF and World Bank agreements intervene illegally are in regulations regarding indigenous communities' land rights, cultural rights, and the right to control their own social, economic and political development. The agreements frequently ignore, subtly or openly, International Labor Organization Convention No. 169 (Concerning Indigenous and Tribal Peoples in Independent Countries). This Convention states that indigenous communities must be consulted when any kind of exploration or exploitation of natural resources is going to be carried out in indigenous ancestral territories. Union rights are also excluded, limited, or ignored, especially the rights of association and mobilization. To protect new companies or their investors from unions that might jeopardize their profits, legislative changes regarding collective bargaining have been introduced that essentially undermine the existence of unions.

Other legal changes include tariff rebates, preferential agreements—which are not applied reciprocally to products produced in our country—tax exemptions, tax parity between national and foreign industries, facilitation of profit repatriation, compensation for nationalization, and special guarantees in the case of lawsuits against transnationals. Cases of litigation between the State and private parties are referred to private arbitration tribunals whose decisions always end up favoring the rights of multinationals over the rights of the nation, resulting in enormous losses for the public treasury.[7]

Plan Colombia and the military cooperation agreements

Occidental Petroleum, other U.S. petroleum companies, European mining companies and others who had financed George W. Bush's presidential campaign lobbied the U.S. Congress for the passage of Plan Colombia. This plan later gave priority to military actions—with the open support of paramilitary groups, U.S. government agencies and mercenaries—in zones where these companies were carrying out their exploitation. Plan Colombia even provided for the construction of three strategically placed "anti-narcotics" bases—all three of them in energy- and mineral-rich zones where foreign companies are trying to gain a foothold. The first, in the South of Bolívar, is located close to one of the most important gold deposits in the world where a violent dispute

A U.S. Army Special Forces soldier teaches counterinsurgency techniques to a Colombian army unit. Photograph by Garry Leech.

is ongoing between small miners and foreign companies. The second, in Norte de Santander, sits alongside the Caño Limón-Coveñas oil pipeline owned by Occidental Petroleum which has been subject to repeated guerrilla attacks. The third, near Ataco, Tolima Department, overlooks important gold and precious metal deposits that have also been the object of U.S. multinational interest and the target of Colombian military/paramilitary operations.

Plan Colombia not only gives priority to military operations. After identifying internal disorder, the Colombian government established "Rehabilitation and Consolidation Zones" suspending civil liberties in several areas of the country. These zones coincided precisely with the trajectory of the Caño Limón-Coveñas pipeline, which passes through the Departments of Arauca, Bolívar and Sucre. Immediately after these were declared Rehabilitation Zones, considerable restrictions were introduced on civil and political rights, with troubling results.[8] Over one thousand arbitrary detentions and several massacres and selective homicides were committed under the shelter of Colombian army operations. All of these actions were aimed against the civilian population in the regions. A similar situation exists in Putumayo, where there have been high levels of activity by mercenaries, agencies of the U.S. government, paramilitaries, and the army. One of the Harken Energy Company's largest gas reserves is located in Putumayo. The province also contains significant deposits of gold, precious metals, uranium, rare earth elements, oil, and gas, and vast biological resources, as well as land for the construction of a canal and for widening the Panamerican highway.

The role of Canadian cooperation and mining investment in the Colombian conflict

Any country or company contemplating foreign investment in an area where there is significant social and economic conflict should weigh the decision carefully. This is especially true in the case of the Canadian government, which has always emphasized, at least rhetorically, the defense of human rights as a state policy. Canada's interventions in the global context have generally been in favor of strengthening legislation that protects and promotes human rights.

Nevertheless, in the case of Colombia specifically, Canada's role has not been so exemplary. Actions by Canada's governmental cooperation agencies like CIDA (Canadian International Development Agency) and CERI (Canadian Energy Research Institute, an NGO representing Canadian-based mining and energy companies), have created situations of conflict of interest with its private mining companies. CIDA-CERI has provided aid in the creation of mining, petroleum and environmental legislation in Colombia, and the multinational companies that provide financial support to CIDA-CERI have been in a position to benefit from the new laws.

According to a high official in Colombia's Ministry of Mines and Energy, CIDA-CERI began its involvement when the 1996-1998 Mining Code was being formulated. This Code was written by a Colombian lawyer connected to the Canadian company Corona Goldfields. She carried out a series of legal maneuvers that were both unethical and illegal, which will be described below, to help Canadian, U.S. and British mining companies take over the gold deposits of the South of Bolívar. A protest campaign that included demonstrations outside the U.S. embassy, the mobilization of five thousand small miners and peasants from the region, and a national and international campaign led by Sintraminercol and Amnesty International prevented the Code from being passed. But the response of the Colombian state, as has been typical in this type of situation, was to begin a military/paramilitary operation in the region, producing serious violations of the human rights of the miners and peasants there.

The business behavior of some Canadian mining companies leaves much to be desired. One diplomat characterized their actions as more appropriate to pirates or buccaneers than to a serious business enterprise. Some companies have manipulated the stock market.[9] Others, like GreyStar, have made promises, under pressure from the guerrillas, to carry out public works in the region for the benefit of the inhabitants. When they failed to carry out these projects, the population protested, and was consequently expelled from the region.[10]

Months after the mine was abandoned, the Colombian army began an operation to allow GreyStar to remove its machinery. This military operation too, according to miners residing on former company property, led to human rights violations of the inhabitants.

The Corona Goldfields company has generated significant conflicts in Marmato, in the Department of Caldas. The company bought some properties from small and medium miners, paying them 50%, and in some cases only 20%, of the agreed-upon value of the lands. The company promised to complete the payment in installments as their mining operations progressed. But four years later it still has not repaid its debts to these miners. Even though they did not receive full payment for their lands, the miners cannot return to them because they gave up their titles, so any mining activity they carried out would be declared illegal. To make matters worse, the small sums that they received have been used up, which means that they cannot reinitiate their mining activities independently. They have always been miners; their livelihoods have depended solely on mining. Now that they cannot get access to the mines they are suffering severe economic hardship, with disastrous effects on their families and the community as a whole.

CIDA-CERI's role in the new mining, petroleum and telecommunications legislation

Based on an agreement signed with the Canadian Cooperation agencies, the Colombian government contracted the law firm of Martínez Córdoba and Associates to fulfill two basic requirements in the formulation of the new Mining Code: to ensure compliance with environmental procedures and carry out consultations with indigenous communities.

The lawyers fulfilled the first objective. But they also served as legislative consultants during the entire period of discussion and approval of the law, and in that role introduced a series of articles in Chapter XXII of the new Mining Code that have had very deleterious effects on environmental management in the mining regions.

With respect to the indigenous communities, these same lawyers later acknowledged in a letter that they never fulfilled their obligation to carry out consultations and negotiate an agreement. They simply sent the chapter on ethnic groups directly to the Congress. That is, the lawyers did not fulfill the contract, nor uphold the law, or the constitution, much less ILO Convention 169, which requires consultation with indigenous groups and which Colombia ratified in 1991 with Law 21.

As we will show below, the Canadian Cooperation agencies had the sole goal of benefiting the companies that make up CERI, to the detriment of the economic, social, and environmental situation of the majority of the Colombian people. CIDA-CERI played the same role in the creation of petroleum legislation. The tax cuts, tax exemptions, lack of environmental controls and the near disappearance of the state petroleum agency, Ecopetrol, brought huge benefits to multinational companies based in Canada. Canadian companies received 73% of the new exploration contracts. Some companies with poor human rights records elsewhere, like Canada's Talisman Energy (which is being sued for illegal operations in Sudan) were even able to increase their holdings.

The new telecommunications legislation also created joint ventures. Nortel and three other multinationals brought about the liquidation of Telecom, the state telecommunications agency. This virtually destroyed of one of the two largest unions in the country when five thousand state workers were terminated. Colombia's economy was severely damaged solely in order to increase the profits of transnational corporations.

Writing a New Mining Code for the Multinationals

The 1996 Mining Code project: Legal maneuvers

The 1996 Mining Code project grew from the need to bring our legislation into line with the new trend of economic globalization that the World Bank was imposing on many Third World countries. These policies attempt to remove the state from its role in the exploitation of mineral resources and make them available to transnational capital at ridiculously low prices.

Colombia's 1996 code has a very peculiar history. In addition to what has already been explained, there has been a shameless, illegal and criminal attempt to take over the gold

A miner in the South of Bolívar. From "Colombia Mining Video" by Sintraminercol.

Children in a mining village in the South of Bolívar. From "Colombia Mining Video" by Sintraminercol.

mines located in the South of Bolívar which, according to very credible technical sources, can be considered one of the largest deposits of gold in the world.

The South of Bolívar is located near the center of Colombia and contains about one fourth of the population of this Department. The Magdalena River flows through it, and it has been a zone of continuous social conflict.

This region produces half of the gold in the country.[11] The town of Río Viejo in this region was, before the paramilitary incursions, the largest gold producer in the country, surpassing even the *municipios* of Antioquia, which have traditionally been the largest producers.[12] Miners who had come from different areas of the Republic fleeing the violence unleashed by the assassination of Jorge Eliécer Gaitán in 1948 settled in the Serranía de San Lucas, in the South of Bolívar, to engage in small-scale artisanal gold mining.

Artisanal mining techniques in the South of Bolívar. From "Colombia Mining Video" by Sintraminercol.

Artisanal mining techniques in the South of Bolívar. From "Colombia Mining Video" by Sintraminercol.

While the miners carried out their small-scale production, an important transaction was taking place. In 1950 Leopoldo Valet sold 10 mines to Juan de Dios Illera. These mines were located "in the jurisdiction of the *municipio* of Simití, Bolívar Province."[13] In the 1970s, after Juan de Dios Illera's death, his descendants began legal action to reclaim the mines, known as Private Property 026. However, they did not even know the location of the mines.[14] They also had no title from the Spanish Crown, nor a judgment from the Council of State (the highest court that handles litigation between individuals and the state), that recognized their ownership. Nor had they ever operated these mines that were supposedly theirs. Thus they fulfilled none of the requirements of Colombian law for the recognition of a mine as private property. The plaintiffs claimed that problems of public order in the zone had prevented them from beginning any exploration or exploitation of the mines. But they were simply covering up the fact that they did not know exactly where the mines were, for prior to 1970, there was no guerrilla presence at all within 200 km of Simití.

Royalty Law 141 of 1994 (a law imposing a royalty or production tax on all petroleum and minerals extracted) gave de facto miners two years to legalize their exploitations. Over 90 mining associations in the South of Bolívar began proceedings to be granted titles and licenses for exploration and exploitation. Many of these were recognized.

Strangely, however, one of the richest mines was not legalized. In a November 20, 1996, official survey form, this mine appears as property of the Illera Palacio family. However, the official who drew up the form made it clear that "the area in question conflicts with other existing petitions for mine legalization" and that "the areas most affected by the

Artisanal mining techniques in the South of Bolívar. From "Colombia Mining Video" by Sintraminercol.

conflicting claims are those called Pájaro Azul, Esperanza, and Las Hojas."[15] These statements demonstrate that the Illera Palacios's claim does not correspond to reality and can never be proven, because it is false.

Another serious discrepancy is that this form claims alluvial mining zones where there are no rivers. Their goal was to have this nonexistent private property entered in the national registry, in order to support negotiations coming from the office of Minister of Mines Rodrigo Villamizar AlvarGonzález. (Villamizar has a long and close relationship with President George W. Bush.[16]) These negotiations began on January 30, 1995. On that date, the Illera Palacio family retained Luisa Fernanda Aramburo Restrepo, a lawyer who worked for Corona Goldfields—a Canadian subsidiary of the U.S. transnational Conquistador Mines—to begin proceedings for the recognition of Private Property 026.

This lawyer knew precisely the quality and quantity of gold in this zone. Since 1994 she had been carrying out another mining project in Norosí, also in the South of Bolívar, representing the Norosí Ltd. Mining Company, owned by a group of North Americans. The lawyer was representing the Illera Palacio family at the same time that she was seeking the recognition of Property 026. Realizing the potential of the deal the multinational she represented could have in its hands, she created a new company called Minera San Lucas Ltd.,[17] with a U.S. citizen named James David Greenbaum (possibly a shareholder in Corona Goldfields), to contract for the exclusive rights to exploit the mines that she was claiming in the name of the Illera Palacios. She then signed a contract with the Illera Palacios, agreeing to the payment of a large sum, in dollars, for the mine.[18] This was entirely unjustified, given that her company was formed with only $500 in capital, which does not support the financial commitment that she made to the Illera Palacios for over $100,000 USD.

In late 1996 the small miners of the Serranía de San Lucas began to receive telegrams asking them to travel to Bucaramanga to meet with representatives of the *owners* of the area known as Private Property 026. Not all of them could travel, and in March 1997 the Minister of Mines Villamizar AlvarGonzález appeared in Santa Rosa with the multinational's lawyer, to "resolve the differences" with the miners and allow the entrance of the multinational that had already signed an agreement with the Illera Palacios. But the attempt failed because the miners studied the documents in the Ministry of Mines and decided to withdraw from the negotiations.

On top of all this, the lawyer created a Temporary Partnership, which was contracted by Villamizar AlvarGonzález, through the UPME (Mining-Energy Planning Unit, part of Colombia's Ministry of Mines and Energy), to design a new Mining Code.[19] The final version of this proposed Code was delivered on April 26, 1996; one day earlier, a paramilitary operation had begun in the South of Bolívar.

We must emphasize that this lawyer was also aided by CERI, with money from CIDA, to draw up the 1999 Mining Code proposal. Aramburo was also the representative of Corona Goldfields (another Canadian company) in its litigation against the small miners of the Serranía de San Lucas.

The projected law included several articles that openly favored the multinational that Attorney Aramburo represents.[20] There are three in particular that, had they been approved, would have unleashed serious problems for the national mining industry. Article 7, which concerns areas in which mining is restricted, eliminated the "excluded" areas where mining was prohibited altogether, and turned them into "restricted" areas, where mining could be carried out if permission was obtained. Thus mining was now allowed in "zones that had been declared National Park, National Reserve, Unique Natural Areas, Flora and Fauna Sanctuaries, and Archeological Zones or Zones of Historical and Cultural Patrimony." Not even the most subservient state in the world would agree to these terms, since they compromise the future of the citizens of the nation and of everyone who inhabits our planet.

The same logic underlies Article 99, "Environmental Legislation Applicable to Mining." This article "excludes the granting of environmental licenses for mining activities" and allows a designated environmental agency to "revise and challenge mining-environmental plans." But since the primary object of interest was the South of Bolívar mines (which were then under litigation because of the maneuvers that had been implemented to take them away from their true owners), the Code introduced a new article, Article 29, which states "In the case that several applications are made for a single area, the first one presented will prevail before the competent authority." With this article the gold mines belonging to the small miners of the Serranía de San Lucas were lost. For the Illera Palacio family (and the multinational) represented by Attorney Aramburo had first presented their claim to RPP 026 in the 1970s, and the miners had not presented their claim until 1995. Thus the first one to present a claim to the competent authority was Corona Goldfields, since they had already signed a contract for exclusive exploitation of the mines in the 1970s.

In addition, in the Fifth Commission of the House of Representatives, a representative of the Department of Bolívar (who has been accused by several human rights organizations of having links to the paramilitaries) introduced a new article that showed clearly what the Colombian state does with its citizens when they demand their rights or oppose the interests of the transnationals. Article 128 was entitled "The Program of Economic Substitution" and it "created a program of economic substitution *to help small miners displaced from their mining activities*" (emphasis added).[21] This article was approved months before the paramilitary operations began to expel the miners who work in these hills. It appears therefore that the State and some legislators knew beforehand what was being planned for the South of Bolívar and its mining zones.

This new Code contained other important elements. Article 105 threatened the existence of the indigenous and Afro-Colombian communities. Other articles ordered the liquidation of the State mining agency, Mineralco, S.A., as a way of ending the state's role in mining production. In their presentation of the proposed legislation, the lawyers stated that privatization had been ordered by the World Bank.

The 1996 Mining Code project:
Impact on the mining populations

On March 3, 1997, as the new Mining Code was being debated in the Colombian Congress, the miners received a letter faxed from Corona Goldfields and signed by Efraín Illera Palacio. The letter stated that the authors were "not interested in sponsoring or collaborating with paramilitary or other armed groups." Forty-five days later the paramilitary operation began that took over the most important gold-producing *municipio*, Río Viejo. One villager was assassinated. Paramilitaries cut off his head, kicked it around and stuck it on a post facing the Serranía de San Lucas. They informed the population that they were coming to the Serranía because what they were interested in was the mines, and that they were planning to get rid of the miners who, they claimed, were collaborating with the guerrillas. The ACCU (Peasant Self-Defense of Córdoba and Urabá, today called the AUC), they said, was establishing a presence to guarantee the entrance of the transnationals which would create jobs, generate development, and pay taxes to the state.[22] On July 20, 1997, after a speech in Cartagena where these acts were denounced, the vice president of Asagromisbol,[23] Orlando Caamaño, was assassinated by paramilitaries in the city of Aguachica (Cesar Province).

After this, paramilitary operations increased in several mining towns: San Pablo, Simití, Santa Rosa del Sur, Pueblito Mejía, Tiquisio, San Blas, Monterrey, Puerto Rico, La Pacha, Morales, Moralito, and Arenal. These operations destroyed

Aftermath of the paramilitary operation in the South of Bolívar. From "Colombia Mining Video" by Sintraminercol.

over ten towns, looted and burned more than a thousand homes and two city halls, massacred over 400 people, raped both women and men and then dismembered them in front of the townspeople. Over 35,000 people were displaced by the violence.

These events led to two massive mobilizations of peasants, miners and inhabitants of the affected towns and adjacent regions (that is, Magdalena Medio). The first was a march to the U.S. Embassy in Bogotá, since Conquistador Mines, the company whose lawyer had led all of the maneuvers to take over the mines from the small producers belonging to the federation Fedeagromisbol, is a U.S.-based company. The second mobilization headed to Barrancabermeja. In Barrancabermeja, after a reception characterized by repression, marginalization and overcrowding, the government of Andrés

Peasant and miner mobilization from the South of Bolívar. From "Colombia Mining Video" by Sintraminercol.

Meeting of Fedeagromisbol in the South of Bolívar. From "Colombia Mining Video" by Sintraminercol.

Pastrana Arango (1998-2002) eventually signed an agreement with the representatives of the march on October 4, 1998, promising to give aid, carry out social investment, protect the displaced, combat the paramilitary groups and try any of its agents who had links with these groups.

Despite this agreement, the result has been complete impunity. The guilty have not been tried even though witnesses and evidence were provided in a timely way and according to established legal procedures. Only days after the accords were signed two of the leaders of the march, Edgar Quiroga and Gildardo Fuentes, were disappeared by the paramilitaries. Their fate remains unknown.

But these mobilizations and accusations finally led the Samper government (1994-1998) to decide to archive the projected Code, and at least temporarily stopped a legislative change that would have been disastrous for the small miners of the South of Bolívar and for all mining in our Republic.

AngloGold withdraws

The AngloGold Company, one of the largest producers of gold in the world, acquired 50% of Conquistador Mines in Colombia on November 5, 1999, and planned to invest US $2,500,000 in exploration.[24] The agreement excluded the zone of Marmato, for Conquistador's only project of real importance was the one in the South of Bolívar, as several shareholders stated in discussions in mining sector internet chatrooms.

That is, even though Conquistador held no title to the land, it was already negotiating the largest gold deposits in Colombia on the international market. When the small miners, in spite of the opposition of the guerrilla forces in the region, proposed an equitable deal to a different multinational in order to collaborate in exploiting these resources, the Minister of Mines Luis Carlos Valenzuela and his Vice Minister Luisa Fernanda Lafourie emphatically opposed this alternative. The alternative would have opened the possibility that miners would not be assassinated nor forced to move just because they happened to reside in one of the richest gold mines in the world. It would also have created a way for multinationals to avoid allying with the paramilitary groups to expel the miners in order to take over their mines illegally. Instead, this deal would have allowed a new company to be created with the participation of the small and medium miners, with an equitable distribution of the earnings among all who participated in the company, as has occurred in other parts of the world.

Faced with this situation, Sintraminercol began an international campaign to warn AngloGold about the irregular dealings that had occurred and the conflictive situation in the South of Bolívar. In response, the company sent three representatives to investigate the situation. The representatives at first believed that Sintraminercol had accused the lawyer Aramburo of being a paramilitary. We explained that we had never made that claim, but we had grave concerns about her actions and about the situation in the region. Apparently AngloGold was awaiting the results of its discussions with Sintraminercol to make a final decision about its involvement. The company was evidently sufficiently alarmed that it decided a few days later to withdraw from its deal with Conquistador.[25] In early 2003, AngloGold once again expressed an interest in exploiting the gold mines of the Serranía de San Lucas, according to several of its shareholders close to the current government of Alvaro Uribe Vélez (2002-2006). Uribe's announcement that he was preparing a special battalion to protect investments in the South of Bolívar region may have encouraged them to renew their interest in the project.

The new mining code, Law 685 of 2001:
A law that consolidates looting

Since the first attempt to change the mining legislation during Ernesto Samper's administration had failed, the new Pastrana administration empowered its Vice Minister (later Minister) of Mines, Luisa Fernanda Lafourie, to contract out the drafting of a new proposal for a Mining Code. In so doing, President Pastrana sidestepped the state contracting law requiring an open bidding process for such contracts.[26]

At the same time, and buoyed by an agreement with the Ministry of Mines, the Canadian organization CERI, with money from CIDA, contracted the same lawyers that the government was using for formulating the new law, Martínez Córdoba and Associates.[27] This law firm represents half of the mining companies inscribed in Colombia's national mining registry,[28] including Cemex, Cementos Diamante de Bucaramanga S.A., Ingeniesa S.A.,[29] Ladrillera Santafé,[30] Concretos Diamante Samper S.A.,[31] and others.

The proposal for the law was presented in the fifth session of the Colombian Senate for its first debate, ignoring Article 154, Clause 4 of Colombia's Constitution which states that if a project involves changes in taxation, it must be presented for debate first in the House of Representatives. The consultation with indigenous communities required by Law 21 of 1991, developed in accord with ILO Convention 169, was not carried out. The new law was taken directly to the legislative bodies after only a pathetic farce of a consultation.

Challenges to the 2001 law

As part of the process of formulating its proposal, the government instructed its lawyers to copy the worst mining legislation in Latin America, that of Chile and Argentina. This generated a debate in Congress on the part of the independent representatives, led by Representative Gustavo Petro Urrego. They challenged the dissolution of the state mining entity Minercol Ltda., as well as the tax reforms that favored the large mining enterprises to such an extreme that the state would receive virtually no returns from any mining in our territory. Other controversial elements included changing the length of mining concessions from 25 to 90 years (through extensions), and granting foreign mining companies exclusive mining titles. In spite of over 300 meetings, the government was willing to change only what didn't favor the transnationals, and sent the project to Congress for the final debates.

Sintraminercol and the Corporation of Land Workers, supported by the Canadian Embassy, Minercol Ltda., Kairos, and environmental and human rights organizations, organized three forums in Bucaramanga, Cali, and Bogotá, with 300 unions from the mining sector. Their resolutions called upon the Congress to halt the projected law and discuss it with indigenous and Afro-Colombian communities, small and medium miners, and other groups involved in this sector of the economy. They added proposals seeking a strong state mining entity that could control and partner with small, medium and large companies. They expressed the need for the state to carry out basic mining exploration in order to really know what was being negotiated, as well as for a strong environmental authority, given that most mining projects are being carried out in areas of very sensitive ecosystems. More generally, the resolutions called for a national policy in defense of the country's resources. There were also strong statements condemning the practice of forced displacement and the violations of human rights in the mining regions. Finally, the government was requested to immediately end paramilitary operations in the mining zones.[32]

None of these calls were heeded. Minercol was first subjected to restructuring, and now its final liquidation is being carried out, which will destroy the remaining unions. The law that was finally approved goes well beyond the mining sector and regulates administrative, penal, labor, civil, and ethnic minority issues. It even affects constitutional issues, and thus has spurred legal action before the Constitutional Court for contradicting this fundamental document that rules this self-proclaimed *estado social de derecho*.[33]

How the 2001 law harms the people of Colombia

The most egregious articles, in economic, social and legal terms, are the following:

- Articles 3 and 4 regarding exclusive regulation attempt to deny the applicability of any laws outside of the code. In response to a lawsuit claiming the unconstitutionality of these articles, the Constitutional Court ruled that "the term *exclusive* does not exclude the application of requirements established by laws that protect the historical, archeological or cultural patrimony of the nation and constitutionally protected rights and goods."[34]

- Article 5 regarding the ownership of resources conflicts with Constitutional guarantees granted to the collective land rights of indigenous and Afro-Colombian communities.

- Article 13, regarding the declaration of public utility, like Article 5, violates the rights of communities by subordinating the fundamental rights of the cultures of different peoples to the application of the so-called principle of public utility, placing the national interest before the interests of indigenous communities.

- Article 14, which concedes exclusive mining title to foreign companies, even in areas owned and administered by the state mining authority, aims at opening all lands to foreign investment.

- Chapter VII extends the length of a concession to 30 years, plus two possible extensions. In conjunction with Article 228 which guarantees the rate of the royalty tax, this Chapter all but eliminates any Colombian state control of mining and its profits.

- Chapter XIV regarding ethnic groups was not discussed with the indigenous communities.[35] The Constitutional Court ruled in Decision C-891 of 2002 that "the mining authorities must fulfill the parameters established with regard to previous consultation" with indigenous groups. This means that the Colombian state is obliged to respect its responsibility to consult with the indigenous groups that will be affected before agreeing to a mining contract.

- Title IV, Chapter XVI, eliminates the difference between small, medium and large mining, obliging the first two to compete under the same conditions as large companies.

- Chapter XVII, regarding illicit exploration and exploitation of mines, criminalizes and disables the small miner who, given the economic conditions and social and armed conflict in our country, is not able to "legalize" his claim.

- Chapter XXII, environmental aspects, is one of the most humiliating ever agreed to by our country. It grants destructive advantages to large companies, disregarding the sensitive environmental condition of our country. Articles 207 and 208 guarantee the class of license and the environmental license for *the entire period of the concession*, not allowing any environmental authority the ability to change this decision, even if there are serious violations of environmental law. Article 210 allows modifications of the license *at the request of the operator* (the mining company). Article 211, Revocation of License, states that the State *can* (not *must*, which should be its legal obligation) revoke the license in cases of *repeated and serious violations* of the company's environmental obligations!!! (Emphasis added.) Finally, this Chapter privatizes environmental auditing, as a gift to Ingeniesa S.A., part of the Holcim group, because prior to this only the State environmental authority could carry out environmental audits.

- Chapter XXII, regarding economic and tax aspects, enacts a tax reform for transnationals. Article 227 stipulates a royalty tax of 0.4% for private exploiters of the subsoil. (Prior to this, private producers operating on state land had to pay, in the case of coal, 10%-15% in royalty taxes, according to the amount produced. This change will be further discussed in the next section.) Article 228 allows a fixed royalty tax for the entire period of operation, including the extensions. Article 229 creates an incompatibility with national, municipal and departmental taxes.[36] Article 231 prohibits new taxes on the industry, no matter how much damage it produces to the environment. Article 233 excludes the mining industry from the norm of prepayment of taxes on estimated earnings, and Article 235 classifies logging as a kind of mining exportation of green (i.e., living) products, and exempts this industry from any type of tax or levy for a period of 30 years.

- Chapter XXIII, Article 256 authorizes securitization.[37] According to information gathered by unions in the financial sector, some Colombian industries have used this process as a way of funneling funds to paramilitary organizations. These unions note that securitization has frequently been used in this way in the cattle industry, one of the main supporters of the paramilitaries in Colombia.

- Chapter XXIV, regarding social aspects of mining, simply makes demagogic promises of help for small miners. This clause has remained entirely inoperative: the first result of this code has been the staggering growth of illegal mining operations.

- Chapter XXV, procedural norms, changes the constitution. According to Article 289 of this chapter, a common citizen cannot legally challenge a mining contract. This article is a clear preemptive move against the lawsuits that are sure to follow these new contracts and concessions because of the harm they will bring to the national interest.

- Article 317, regarding mining authority, converts the Ministry of Mines into the sole mining authority, leaving Minercol Ltda. as a public establishment, and not as an industrial and commercial state entity. This essentially guarantees its liquidation.

- Article 321 eliminates the state role in environmental assessment, creating external environmental auditors. This leaves the decisions regarding the ecosystem of the mining regions in the hands of private capital.

Colombia's Constitutional Court, in its decisions C-339/02, C-418/02, C-614/02, C-891/02, and C-978/02 concerning the Mining Code, upheld some articles and gave conditional approval to others; the Court declined to rule on some sections. The Siempre Viva Corporation, the José Alvear Restrepo Lawyers' Collective, and Sintraminercol are pursuing further legal action seeking to have the entire text declared unconstitutional. We believe that the law violates the premises of the *estado social de derecho* decreed by Colombia's 1991 Constitution.

The Royalty Tax:
Is it unconstitutional to tax multinationals?

Colombian law requires enterprises exploiting non-renewable resources in the country to pay a royalty tax on production. According to Article 5 of Law 619 of 2000, "in the case of the exploitation of non-renewable natural resources in the subsoil of private property, the owner of the subsoil will pay the percentage equivalent to that established as royalty tax by Article 16 of Law 141 of 1994"—in the case of coal, 10%-15% (depending on the amount of coal produced). This provision required the multinational Carbones Colombianos del Cerrejón S.A. to pay the tax on all coal exported from Colombia. On February 5, 2001, the company's lawyer Alfonso Gómez Rengifo requested that the Ministry of Mines find a way to exempt it from the tax by declaring the article unconstitutional.[38]

Carlos Caballero Argáez, who was Minister at the time, had already received an offer on January 24, 2001, from tax lawyer Lucy Cruz de Quiñones, to analyze the possibility of declaring Article 5 unconstitutional. The Minister contracted her on February 6, and that same day she presented him with her opinion, which of course supported the claim of unconstitutionality. The Minister immediately ordered Minercol Ltda. to exempt Carbones Colombianos del Cerrejón from the royalty tax and allow it to export without paying any royalties. The Nation thus lost three million dollars through an arbitrary and illegal act with no basis in law or jurisprudence.

The head of the Ministry's Legal Office, Mónica Hilarión Madariaga, and her aide María Clemencia Díaz López, proceeded to endorse *all* of the challenges against this article presented by lawyers connected to the big companies in the mining sector, basing their decision on Cruz de Quiñones's opinion and the Carbones Colombianos case regarding the unconstitutionality of Article 5.[39] The state representatives, instead of protecting the economic interests of the state, protect those of the multinationals.

On July 11, 2001, the Constitutional Court announced its decision, designated C-737/01. The court declared the Law 619/2000 inadmissible, but deferred its effective invalidation until June 20, 2002, giving the Colombian Congress until that date to replace it with new legislation. But in October 2001, on the last day of debate on the revised Mining Code in the House of Representatives, a new clause was introduced in Article 227 stating "private owners of the subsoil will pay no less than 0.4% of the value of the production calculated or measured upon exiting the mine (that is, before any processing has occurred), to be paid in cash or in kind."

Private producers of subsoil resources received a huge boon with this maneuver, which neatly took care of their concerns with the obligations imposed by the Court's ruling. They would have to pay the tax, but only at the new 0.4% rate. A few days later the Minister of Mines and President Pastrana signed Decree 2353 of November 1, 2001, modified on January 2, 2002, setting the maximum amount of the royalty tax at 0.4%, payable in mining infrastructure or minerals. With the stroke of a pen, once again the Nation lost enormous sums of money which could have been used to address social problems, like the fact that 80 children in Colombia perish every day from hunger, malnutrition, and curable diseases.[40]

Predictably (and this is why Article 227 was introduced), two months after Law 685/2001 came into effect, President Pastrana Arango signed a contract for the exploitation of Cerrejón Zona Media, Mina Patilla, with the Glencore company, with the new royalty tax of 0.4%. As we have stated, this amount means that our country will receive virtually no economic return from the development of this coal project, nor from any other mining project on private property. Only the legal and paramilitary force of the multinationals could have brought about such an injustice.

The Military/Paramilitary Response Against the Population

United States: Military aid against drug trafficking, or a counterinsurgency project to guarantee mining and petroleum investments?

As mentioned above, in April 1999 in Cartagena de Indias, Clinton's Secretary of Energy Bill Richardson spoke before investors from the United States, Canada, and other countries. He expressed his government's willingness to use military aid to support the investments that they and their allies were going to make in Colombia, especially in strategically important sectors like mining and energy.

This was not the first time that the U.S. government expressed its interest in mining. On July 27, 1998, the U.S. Embassy in Colombia sent a letter to the director of Mineralco S.A. stating that "The Commercial Section of the U.S. Embassy is preparing a study of the mining sector in Colombia. In view of the country's potential mineral deposits, and the Colombian government's interest in attracting foreign investment to this sector, we are seeking information that will allow us to prepare monographs on the various minerals, as well as lists of companies that are currently developing mining operations in Colombia."[41]

The U.S. government also showed its interest in this sector when it signed the first agreements of its Plan Colombia with the Pastrana government in July 2000. It called for the construction of "three antinarcotics military bases," all of them in important mining and energy regions.[42]

The first base is in the South of Bolívar, home to one of the most important gold deposits in the world (see map 2). The U.S.-based company Conquistador Mines (today Platinum Western) has been litigating for the largest gold mine in the Americas there, along with the AngloGold company. The Harken Energy Company, in which the Bush family is a shareholder, is currently exploring oil deposits in this region. The Caño Limón-Coveñas oil pipeline, operated by Occidental Petroleum, a company that lobbied heavily for Plan Colombia, also goes through this area, one of the largest gas and oil reserves in Colombia.

The second is in the area of Catatumbo, in the Department of Norte de Santander, another region that the Caño Limón-Coveñas pipeline passes through (see map 1). The Uribe government also declared several zones of the country as "rehabilitation zones" for this company, in which the army, the paramilitaries, and mercenaries protect its infrastructure. Their actions seriously violate the human rights of the inhabitants, as demonstrated by a report by the Cinep and Justicia y Paz database in 2003.[43] There are also huge coal deposits in Norte de Santander, and 90% of the coal produced in the region is bought by U.S. companies, for use in the U.S. steel industry. Recent reports show that a British company associated with high officials in Alvaro Uribe's government is also interested in this coal.

The third base is in Ataco, Department of Tolima. U.S. multinationals are especially interested in this region because it contains important gold and precious metal deposits, especially near the town of Río Blanco. Since 2000 there has been a growing paramilitary operation in the region against peasants and miners focusing on the area around Río Blanco—the region with the highest rate of displacement in the department, and one of the highest rates in the country.

Let us examine other coal mining zones, like El Paso and Jagua de Ibirico in the Department of Cesar, where the U.S.-based Drummond Company currently operates. These regions have suffered paramilitary campaigns since 1985, even before the exploration phase began. The paramilitary groups remain in the zone and have continually attacked the

Drummond workers' union, Sintramienergética, killing six of its members.[44] Paramilitaries control the area around the mine, the nearby towns, and all of the roads that Drummond uses to transport workers and coal.

Another high priority investment zone for the United States and its allies is in the Departments of Putumayo and Chocó. Putumayo contains not only gold and precious metals, but also copper-molybdenum and rare earth elements.[45] It also contains huge natural gas wells that Harken Energy, a company in which the Bush family holds a large number of shares, is interested in.

Recently the Colombian government has been accused of proposing legislation to raise the internal prices of natural gas and to allow for its export to make it more profitable.[46] The government and several parliamentarians presented this legislation with the goal of favoring the U.S. president's company (Harken Energy) to the detriment of Colombia's need to collect tax revenues. Independent members of Congress in Colombia denounced this fact and the legislation died in Congress.

Other regions containing strategic deposits of gold and other precious metals have also suffered foreign intervention, like the so-called "state reserve"[47] 1227 in Taraira-La Pedrera in the Department of Vaupés.[48] Other mineral-rich areas where violence has increased include state reserve 1236 of gold/precious metals in Río Sucio in the Antioquia Atrato; 1194 in the Serranía de Naquén in the Department of Guainía, and state reserve 1313 in San Juan, Department of Chocó. A strong and controlling paramilitary presence has also appeared in areas around other mineral deposits, like the ferronickel deposits in the Department of Córdoba, and the limestone deposits in Yumbo and Vijes, in the Department of Valle del Cauca (see map 2).

There is yet another twist to this story. As in most of Colombia's territory, there are cultivations of coca and poppy for illicit use in these mineral-rich areas. Plan Colombia, which in theory aims to combat the cultivation, production, and export of drugs, in fact seeks and achieves a huge military cover for the positioning of paramilitaries, who are ultimately in charge of protecting the interests of the U.S. companies. They can carry out war crimes and crimes against humanity without damaging the "honor and integrity" of the Colombian Army.[49]

This is the reason for the huge U.S. government commitment to its agencies and the mercenaries they contract to "combat drug traffic." Many of these mercenaries end up dying in combat against the guerrillas, or of overdoses, like the U.S. mercenary who died at the Larandia military base of an overdose of morphine and heroin, drugs that he was supposedly combating.[50] Some even end up becoming drug traffickers. The DynCorp company, charged with the fumigation of coca and poppy fields, has also been caught exporting drugs.[51] One high U.S. army official, charged with "combating drugs," actually used the U.S. Embassy diplomatic pouch to send drugs to the United States.[52]

Paramilitaries, mercenaries, U.S. government agencies, and the "security" of the multinationals

It is no secret that since Vietnam the United States has created groups of paramilitaries. In Latin America, these were first used in the southern cone dictatorships, and later in Central America, where under the name of "death squads" they killed over half a million Salvadorans, Guatemalans, Hondurans and

Colombian paramilitaries at AUC camp near La Dorada, Putumayo.
Photograph by Garry Leech.

Nicaraguans. For citizens of these countries, and especially for the Maya of Guatemala, it is no secret that the Reagan Administration financed and trained these paramilitaries.[53]

In the Colombian case, the idea has always circulated that the paramilitaries were created by the drug traffic mafia. This is a half-truth. In his confession before the public prosecutor and to human rights organizations, a paramilitary chief nicknamed "black Vladimir" stated that in the meetings the paramilitaries held with soldiers stationed with the Puerto Boyacá Battalion, in the Department of Boyacá, there were representatives of the Texas Petroleum Company in addition to ranchers, mafiosos and small industrialists, and that all of these paid the U.S., Israeli and English mercenaries who trained them.[54]

Foreign businesses have not been the only outsiders supporting these groups. The U.S. government is also implicated, as revealed in "Colombia's Killer Networks," a report by Human Rights Watch. The networks used U.S. funds

Ecopetrol oil refinery in Barrancabermeja. Photograph by Jim Harney.

destined for the "drug wars" to create an intelligence network in the Colombian Navy, which ended up killing over 350 social and union leaders in the petroleum port of Barrancabermeja, among them Manuel Gustavo Chacón, an important leader of the petroleum workers.[55]

The situation in the petroleum sector is as critical as that in the mining sector. The two coincide geographically (see map 2). U.S. government agencies play a decisive role, as shown by the following facts. In November 1999, the President of Panama, Mireya Moscoso, publicly asked the CIA to stop stealing Panamanian helicopters in order to give them to Colombian paramilitaries.[56] This statement was made after an active officer of the Colombian Army was detained trying to steal a Panamanian helicopter.

Four months later, a paramilitary operation began in San Pedro Frío, Serranía de San Lucas, the location of the mine under litigation between Conquistador Mines and the small miners. One of the helicopters stolen by the CIA in Panama appeared in this operation, picking up paramilitaries and bombing the population, in a nationally televised news report.[57]

When a human rights organization in the region was informed of this fact, it confirmed the presence of another helicopter of the same model and size in the Catatumbo region, where the U.S. company Occidental Petroleum operates, and where the DEA is planning another "anti-drug" base.

Our research team has found evidence that the CIA and the DEA have provided more than just helicopters to the paramilitary groups.[58] They have also provided arms in operations that have been reported in Colombian newspapers. For example, they provided 7,000 guns, 500 of which have ended up in the South of Bolívar, so that the AUC, a group of mercenaries, and the Colombian army could maintain a criminal siege of the population, preventing the entrance of food, medicine, or medical personnel, forcing residents to leave and clearing the way for the entrance of U.S. multinationals.

It is also public knowledge that CIA agents have "negotiated" reduced sentences with Colombian drug traffickers, with whom they have old and strong relations, in exchange for the delivery of large sums of money to the U.S. government.[59] As drug trafficker Fabio Ochoa pointed out, this money ends up supporting the paramilitaries.[60] Ochoa was extradited to the United States when he refused to give $30 million to the paramilitaries.

This evidence shows how the U.S. government, its agencies and its mercenaries are at the root of the process of positioning regular and irregular (paramilitary) forces around the mining and energy mega-projects. The Drug Wars are no more than a cover for the true, aggressive and criminal intentions of those in the government who develop social and economic policies for our country. Thus it is no coincidence what Phillip Chicola, head of the U.S. State Department's Office of Andean Affairs, said as he began to lead a campaign to repay the favors that the paramilitaries have done for the U.S. government and its corporations: The paramilitary forces, he stated, "are at some moment going to have to be part of a [peace] process, and I think the Colombian government and Colombian society are going to have to decide how to manage this issue."[61] Recently the Uribe government has initiated a process of reinsertion for the paramilitaries, led and supported by the government of the United States.

State financing: Gold production and the royalty tax

In this section we would like to emphasize how the Colombian state contributes to the machinations of these paramilitary groups, which it calls "outside the law." One of the most subtle methods is the fictitious declaration of gold production in departments and *municipios* where the paramilitaries have the greatest presence and are carrying out their political-military project, along with the transnationals that are stealing our resources.

If we follow the production of gold from 1990 to 2000, the Department of Córdoba, headquarters of the so-called AUC (United Self-Defense of Colombia), which had never produced more than 1.7 tons of gold per year, shows an extraordinary increase after 1997—when the paramilitary operation in the South of Bolívar entered full force (see fig. 1). (The operation had already begun in the Department of Antioquía.) In 1997

Córdoba produced three times as much gold as in previous years, and in 1998 this number was multiplied by seven. However, there is absolutely no evidence of new deposits or any large exploitation that could produce such results.

This phenomenon has an explanation, however. Our legislation requires gold producers to pay a royalty tax of 4% to the *municipio* where the gold is produced (see fig. 2). This tax goes to the Fondo Nacional de Regalías (the National Royalties Fund),[62] which transfers it to the *muncipios* and departments to be used primarily for infrastructure: the building of roads, aqueducts, hospitals, etc. But frequently these resources end up in the hands of corrupt officials[63] who share them with groups of drug traffickers and in the end with the paramilitaries. The paramilitaries use the money to buy weapons and consolidate their zones of operation politically. What is happening, therefore, is that these royalties are ending up in the hands of one of the parties in the armed conflict, with the approval of the state. There have even been popular uprisings against certain mayors because of this diversion of funds, as was the case recently in the *municipio* of Montelíbano, in Córdoba, one of the largest recipients of royalties from gold production in the region.

Multinationals Sued for Conspiracy with Paramilitaries and for the Extermination of the Population

The Drummond case

Sintramienergética has sued the Drummond Coal Company, a U.S. company based in Alabama, for conspiring with paramiltiary groups to exterminate the union. This suit was brought after years of abuses ranging from forcing potential employees to undergo lie detector tests to reveal their political affiliation as a condition of employment, to the assassination of union leaders, their displacement from the mining zones, and accusations made against them of being guerrilla supporters.

With the beginning of the company's explorations in Cesar province came the first massacres, the first forced displacements, selective homicides and destruction of the social fabric organized around guilds, unions, political movements, NGOs, etc.[64] When the company began mining operations, the zone had been *consolidated* and the military/paramilitaries took control of the mining zone, the adjacent region, and the area where the railroad was built to carry the coal from the mine to the port. The company and the paramilitaries stayed, and their operations against the union began immediately. Although union leaders brought repeated pleas for security to the management of the company, including Ricardo Urbina, Pedro Maya, and Augusto Jiménez, president of the La Loma Mine, and even to Garry Drummond, owner of the company, they got no response.[65] On March 12th 2001, Valmore Locarno Rodríguez and Víctor Hugo Orcasita Amaya, the President and Vice President of the union local, were taken

Garry Drummond owns a Coal Company in Colombia...

Garry Drummond is getting richer.

These men wanted safer working conditions and better pay for the workers...

Gustavo **SOLER**   Valmore **LOCARNO Rodriguez**   Víctor Hugo **ORCASITA**

Because they were unionists, they were tortured and murdered.

Stop Corporate Terrorism in Colombia.

www.drummondwatch.org

Poster featuring union leaders Victor Hugo Orcasita, Valmore Locarno and Gustavo Soler. Photographs courtesy of Sintramienergética.

The Drummond comapny's cheerful logo "Drumino" contrasts with the pattern of assassination of union organizers at its Colombian mine. Artwork by Terry Burke.

from a company bus en route from the mine to their homes. Locarno was assassinated with two shots in the head in front of his coworkers. Over the protests of the workers, Orcasita was taken away in a truck. The next day his body was found, with obvious signs of torture. On October 5th of the same year, under similar circumstances, Gustavo Soler, the union's new president, was taken from a bus, taken away in a pick-up, tortured, and killed. His body was found on October 7th by people from the area.

The multinationals follow a standard procedure. They sign a security contract with the Colombian army to receive protection, especially from attacks by the guerrillas. But this agreement is, literally, an agreement with the paramilitaries, given their symbiotic relationship. These groups of *armed civilians* were created by Law 48 of 1968, later disbanded, but reconstituted in the 1980s. The current president of Colombia, Alvaro Uribe Vélez, when he was governor of Antioquia, legalized them again, calling them Convivir Security Cooperatives. They were later banned again, but they have continued to operate along with the army with the support of military aid from the United States, Great Britain, Israel, and Spain, among others. A trusted company official coordinates them, providing arms, munitions, money for uniforms, communications equipment, gasoline, vehicles, etc., all under the auspices of this agreement. In some cases, businesses use private security companies made up of ex-officers from the Colombian Army, in conjunction with international security companies that use English, South African, Israeli, and U.S. mercenaries. Once the collaboration is established, operations are begun mainly against civic leaders, unionists, human rights workers, and even public officials who refuse to cooperate with the company.

In April 2003, the U.S. District Court in Alabama

hearing the case against Drummond allowed the suit brought by Sintramienergética and the relatives of those killed to go forward. The court ruled that Sintramienergética has standing to bring suit against Garry Drummond and the Colombian managers of the company under the Alien Torts Claims Act.[66] The crimes committed violate ILO pacts and agreements, and are also crimes against humanity and war crimes, according to U.S. and international law.

Occidental Petroleum and AirScan

A consistent practice of the multinationals in Colombia is to contract companies and mercenaries to provide "security" during their operations.[67] Occidental Petroleum is no exception: the company contracted mercenaries who flew Skymaster planes belonging to AirScan International, Inc., a private Florida-based security company, to patrol the Caño Limón-Coveñas pipeline, which had suffered continued attacks by the guerrillas.

These operations used helicopters, bombs, and weapons provided by the U.S. "antinarcotics" programs. These programs do not attack the drug cartels, as one might imagine. Instead, they protect the interests of U.S. multinationals. In the case of Santo Domingo, a town in the *municipio* of Tame in Arauca Department where the company operates, they attacked the inhabitants and violated their right to life.

On the morning of December 13 1998, after two days of fierce combat between the army protecting Occidental Petroleum and the FARC in the region of Santo Domingo, the Colombian Army attacked the village of Santo Domingo with air-to-surface rockets and cluster bombs. The bombing left seventeen civilians dead, including seven children, three of them children of Matilde Peñalosa, a resident of Santo

Oil spill from the Caño Limón-Coveñas pipeline in Arauca, after ELN guerrilla attack, 2002. Photograph by Marc Becker.

Domingo. Xiomara Díaz and Luis Rodríguez testified that on the night of December 12 they heard aircraft overflights and machine gun fire in the region. The next day, December 13th, at 9:45 am, they saw a bright light coming from a helicopter, then a trail of smoke, and finally an explosion that threw them to the ground. When they got up and looked around they saw a number of people dead, others injured, and several houses destroyed.

Initially, Air Force General Fabio Velasco denied to the media that planes had fired on civilians. Later, faced with evidence presented by the public prosecutor, he changed his story, claiming that his troops had opened fire against a car that was carrying guerrillas and was loaded with a bomb. When the car was shot, he said, the bomb exploded and killed

Displaced villagers from Tame, Arauca, 2002. Photograph by Marc Becker.

the bystanders. Months later, César Romero, the pilot of the helicopter that dropped the bombs, testified before a military judge that he had carried cluster bombs, rockets and munitions, and that the three mercenaries commanding the Skymaster spy plane had located and indicated the targets and ordered the release of the bombs. He further testified that the decision about the need to bomb the area signaled by the mercenaries had been made hours ahead of time at the military base inside Occidental Petroleum's property.[68]

Reports by the state petroleum company Ecopetrol indicate that Occidental Petroleum pays for the Skymaster planes' services to provide security for their installations and the pipeline. Sintraminercol has been compiling a list of the violations of human rights occurring in the zone around the pipeline. Information collected up to the present show a policy of permanent aggression against these rights on the part of the military/paramilitaries and the mercenaries.

In September 2000 an International Tribunal was held in Chicago regarding this case. In December of the same year, in Saravena, Arauca, hundreds of residents and social organizations heard the Tribunal's conclusions that found Occidental Petroleum, AirScan, the Colombian state, and Generals Fabio Velasco of the Air Force and Hernando Barbosa of the Army responsible for the attacks. The decision also called for these crimes to be judged in civil, rather than military court, for comprehensive reparations to the victims, special aid for the children, the immediate suspension of military support for the units involved in these acts, in accordance with U.S. law, and a suspension of the human rights certification required for the approval of U.S. aid through Plan Colombia. These crimes, which have remained unpunished in Colombia, were brought before a Federal Court in California in April 2003.

The Effects of these Policies on the Colombian Population

First: Colossal corruption

One of the main causes of our country's unfortunate situation is the corruption of a few, who gain great advantages and earn easy money at the cost of the lives of millions of human beings. This kind of behavior has led the countries of the third world to their current state of prostration. Their natural resources are controlled by multinationals, while members of their elite funnel their money to tax havens like the Cayman Islands, the Virgin Islands, Switzerland, and others. Most grievously of all, the great majority of the population lives in grinding poverty.

Economic consequences:

- Colombia has lost over $10.5 billion in the Cerrejón Zona Norte project.[69]

- The Drummond coal mine owes Minercol, Ltda. 48 billion pesos (as of September 2003), in addition to $800,000 that the state lost to Drummond in an Arbitration Tribunal.

- The Colombian government has forgiven over $1.4 million in debts incurred by Colombian mine operators.

- Corruption by high officials in the operations of mining sector companies has cost the state over $400 million.

- Losses from the privatization of Cerro Matoso come to over $74 million. Added to losses assumed by the state when the company was sold to BHP Billiton, this raises the total losses to over $300 million.

- Colombia will lose another $800 million over the next

ninety years that Glencore operates in El Cerrejón Zona Media, if the company continues to produce coal at a rate of 5 million tons/year, because of the reduction of the royalty tax from 10%-15% to .04%. If the company, as is plausible, doubles or triples its production, the losses will be proportionally greater.

- In the last five years, Exxon incurred $600 million worth of losses for Colombia in its operation of the El Cerrejón coal mine, according to the Office of the Comptroller.

- The operational losses from the three large mining projects (El Cerrejón, La Loma, operated by Drummond, and Montelíbano, which produces ferronickel) for our country come to more than $12 billion.

- Just $10 billion would be enough to provide employment for Colombia's three million unemployed, to save the lives of the up to 160 children who die daily of hunger, malnutrition and curable diseases, and to have avoided the closing of over 20 hospitals around the country, which has created a humanitarian emergency in the poorest sectors of the population.

Social consequences:

- 64% of Colombia's population lives below the poverty line (earning less than $3 a day), and 23.4% in absolute poverty (earning less than $2 a day). The mining districts have the highest rates of poverty in the country.

- One in four Colombians does not earn enough to provide the basic food basket. Only 51% of the population is covered by the basic health system. Only 29% are covered by pensions (where those who earn the most contribute the least). The school drop out rate is 17.5%. According to official figures, 82.5% of Colombia's children have access to secondary education (in fact the number is much lower), and only 22.5% have access to higher education.

- Unemployment has risen from 10.6% in 1991 to 20.5% in 2000.[70] Recovering the losses from the Cerrejón Zona Norte mine from the period in which it was operated by Exxon would allow the country to provide work to the three million Colombians who are unemployed.[71]

- 1.8% of the population owns 53% of the land, five economic groups control most of the country's wealth, ten companies comprise 75% of the financial market, and the media—which continually legitimize the extermination of the poor—are in the hands of two powerful economic groups.

- Land has been concentrated by means of violence, forced displacement, and the use of illicit money.

- The Gini coefficient rose from 0.54 to 0.566 in 1999, above the Latin American average. Military spending uses 5% of the country's GDP.[72]

- Although the environmental impact of large mining has not been precisely documented, its consequences are apparent in the health of the Wayuu indigenous community and the deterioration of the biological and physical environment of the mining regions in the Guajira, Cesar, and Córdoba.

- There are 3.5 million children out of school, and the most critical situation is in the mining zones of Chocó, Bolívar and Sucre.[73]

- Eleven million Colombians survive on less than one dollar a day. Over 65% of these live in the mining zones.[74]

Environmental consequences:[75]

- The cutting of forests, diversion of water sources, and the massive movements of earth produced by the Cerrejón Zona Norte mine have diminished the availability of clean water for the inhabitants and for the pasturing of animals, one of the few sources of work for the Afro-Colombians and indigenous Wayuu of the region.

- The region of the Guajira is undergoing an accelerated desertification with the disappearance of forests, land, and water sources, due to the increase in coal production.

- The inhabitants of the villages of Tabaco and Roche, located on the periphery of the mine, have presented evidence of the contamination of rivers, creeks and brooks, as well as contamination of the air that has especially affected children and the elderly. They have also documented a decline in the population of wild animals for hunting, a decline in the number of fish, and impacts on domestic animals, due to the explosions and the dust produced by the mine.

Human rights violations:

- 35,000 people have been forcibly displaced from the South of Bolívar, and so far there have been 535 registered homicides, as a result of the paramilitary operations of the Colombian and U.S. governments (see figs. 3 to 7).

- According to our human rights department, over two

Refugee from the violence, 2002. Photograph by Marc Becker.

million of the country's displaced people come from mining regions (see figs. 3 to 6).

- The homicide rate in Antioquia Department during the time that Colombia's current president, Alvaro Uribe, was governor there rose between 300% and 500% more than other departments with similar demographics (see fig. 7).

- In the mining municipalities, on average, between 1995 and 2002, there have been 828 homicides, 142 forced disappearances, 117 people injured, 71 people tortured, 355 death threats, and 150 arbitrary detentions, every year. In addition there have been 433 massacres, which when added to the homicides give a total figure of 6,626 homicides during those eight years (see fig. 9).[76]

- 68% of the forced displacement in the country occurs in the mining zones.[77] The greatest number of displacements occurred in the mining *municipios* of Río Blanco-Ataco in Tolima, La Gabarra and surrounding areas in Norte de Santander, the *municipios* of the South of Bolívar, and Barrancabermeja in Santander.

- In 1996 and 2001, when the new mining codes were being written, there was a huge increase in human rights violations in the zones affected by the legislation. In Bolívar, for example, there was a 1000% increase in homicides, forced disappearances, injuries, torture, and arbitrary detentions. In 2001, the number of homicides in mining municipalities doubled, to 1667, from the average calculated between 1995 and 2002 (see fig. 9).

- Between 1997 and 1998, forced displacements in the South of Bolívar grew by 1500%, as the paramilitary operation was implemented.

- In 2002 homicides decreased, but the number of arbitrary detentions rose to 2,300. These detentions were later reflected in the figures for extrajudicial executions and forced disappearance (see fig. 9).

- The departments that showed the highest increase in human rights violations were also those that with the greatest concentration of mining operations: Antioquia, Bolívar, Norte de Santander, Santander, and Cesar. Others with high levels of oil and gas production, like Arauca and Putumayo, show the same rates.

- 42% of human rights violations against unionists, in proportion to numbers of workers unionized, occur in the mining-energy sector.

- Approximately one union leader is assassinated each month in the mining-energy sector, according to the human rights department of the CUT.

- Over the past fifteen years in Colombia, a union leader has been assassinated every other day. During the current government of Alvaro Uribe Vélez the number has fallen slightly, to one every five days. In the past year, arbitrary detentions rose approximately 1,500%.

- 97% of the homicides against unionists are committed by the military and paramilitary groups, with the other 3% being committed by the guerrillas and other armed actors.[78]

- Since its founding, the oil workers union Unión Sindical Obrera has seen 81 of its leaders assassinated and over 100 illegal detentions. The ex-president of the union, Hernando Hernández, remains in detention. He was arrested during the process of privatization of Ecopetrol, the state petroleum entity, and the turnover of its assets to the multinationals that helped write the new petroleum legislation.

- Since Alvaro Uribe Vélez's government has come into office, an indigenous person has been assassinated every five days, most of these in areas of natural resource exploitation.

- The new antiterrorist statute effectively closes democratic possibilities of expression, limits civil liberties (as in the rehabilitation zones), limits unions' right to organize and mobilize, prevents the creation of new political organizations, and limits those which already exist.

By Way of Conclusion

1. The strategy of the application of the neoliberal model in Colombia, and the preparation for the imposition of the Free Trade Area of the Americas (FTAA), are being carried out with methods that range from simple violations of fundamental human rights to war crimes and crimes against humanity.

2. The Colombian State, the U.S. Government, their armies, their paramilitaries, their mercenaries, their agencies, their diplomatic officers, their multinationals, and the executives of these multinationals, are the main forces responsible for the violations of human rights in the mining and petroleum regions. Many of these violations have been noted and described in this report. Sintraminercol also notes that the governments of Canada, Japan, and Spain, have begun to take a partisan role in the Colombian civil war, as they give military aid to support agreements against the "terrorism" of one side, but do not do anything to stop the involvement of their own multinationals in terror and violence.

3. With the help of "military aid" agreements, the Colombian government carries out all kinds of legal and illegal actions to "guarantee" foreign investment, at the cost of the human rights of the civilian population, the country's independence and sovereignty and its very existence as an *estado social de derecho* as defined by the 1991 Constitution.

4. The multinationals and the governments of the countries mentioned in this report have written or

lobbied for petroleum, mining, environmental, and telecommunications legislation in Colombia to favor their companies. In some cases these companies already operate in our territory; in other cases they have begun operations as soon as the legislation is changed. One concrete case is the Canadian petroleum companies that signed new agreements for exploration right after the laws for this sector were changed by lawyers affiliated with these companies. The same situation has occurred in the mining sector with U.S. companies.

5. The legislative changes abolish state control over the exploration, exploitation, and sale of resources and in such sensitive areas as the environment, the rights of ethnic groups, workers' rights, and tax policy. They also prevent the application of national and international norms that protect fundamental rights, and they infringe on Colombia's national sovereignty.

6. While there are some exceptional multinationals and transnationals that do not abuse the fundamental rights inscribed in the law, the constitution, and the international agreements and treaties that Colombia has signed, the majority of companies violate these protective norms frequently, flagrantly, and continually.

Sintraminercol and the organizations that support it request:

Of the United Nations, its immediate and effective intervention to end these kinds of violations and impose measures and sanctions to control this type of abuse. That it bring together representatives of all of the companies that operate or intend to operate in our country to ask them to commit publicly to respecting the fundamental rights of the civilian population and its organizations, to not finance any irregular forces, and to respect and not intervene in the legislation of any member country of the United Nations.

Of the International Labor Organization, that it take the measures necessary to put an immediate end to the violations of labor law and international agreements, to stop the Colombian state from carrying out massacres of workers, and to impose immediate sanctions on the multinational companies that one way or another violate labor rights.

Of the Congress of the United States, that it investigate and sanction the criminal actions of U.S. agencies, diplomatic personnel, and multinationals in Colombia.

Of the Government of the United States, that it immediately halt all military aid that is directed to the zones where its multinationals operate or intend to operate. That it facilitate legal action against agents of its multinationals that commit human rights violations, and that it work with national and international human rights organizations to bring those who have committed human rights abuses against the inhabitants of the zones described in this report before an international judicial body.

Of the governments of Canada, Japan, and Spain, that they refuse to get involved in the civil war in Colombia, which has its origins in the profound social and economic inequalities of our country, and will not be resolved by military means. We call on the government of Canada to take a stand in favor of social and political peace in our country, following in the path of ex-Ambassador Guill Rishchynski, whose interventions in favor of a political solution to the Colombian conflict we will always remember with gratitude.

Of the multinational and transnational companies, that they immediately cease all violations of human rights of the inhabitants and workers in the mining and petroleum zones. That they invest in accordance with principles of ethics and social justice, so as not to deepen the profound social inequalities, poverty, misery, and violence in which the majority of Colombians live.

Of the guerrilla organizations, that they respect the norms of war and that they strictly comply with international humanitarian law and the calls of the international community to protect vulnerable sectors of the population, like children and the elderly, from involvement in the war.

Of national and international non-governmental organizations, national and foreign unions, the international community, intellectuals, artists, students, and all of humanity, that they join us in denouncing these acts, calling for justice and reparations, and that they keep a permanent watch to ensure that this type of criminal behavior is immediately halted in our country, our continent, and our planet.

We hold the Colombian government, the U.S. government, and U.S. multinationals responsible for any attack against the personal integrity or the life of any member of our union, our federation, or any of the other NGOs, social organizations or unions that have supported this investigation.

Appendix I

JORGE ORTEGA GARCIA AND ORLANDO CAAMAÑO CAMPAIGN FOR THE DEFENSE OF HUMAN RIGHTS OF THE MINING AND PETROLEUM POPULATIONS

- National campaign protesting the violations of human rights of the inhabitants and workers in mining regions

- Legal challenge to the Mining Code before Colombia's Constitutional Court

- National and international press conference to launch the campaign

- Advertisements in large circulation newspapers in countries where the multinationals are headquartered, showing the humanitarian crisis created by the Colombian government and the companies in the mining and energy sector

- Letter-writing campaign to the U.S. Attorney General demanding that companies that collaborate with terrorist groups be tried and punished

- Legal action against Conquistador Mines, Drummond and Exxon for grave abuses of human rights against the population and workers in the mining regions

- Permanent campaign involving foreign parliaments and governments, NGOs, mass media, political groups and parties, the anti-globalization movement, the environmental movement, embassies, etc., to pressure for no investment in mining unless the state and the multinationals guarantee total respect for the human rights of the population and workers in the mining regions

- Demand that the Governments of Colombia comply with the recommendations and petitions expressed in this document. Call upon the entire international community to support the social and union organizations that are suffering from these violations

For further information about the campaign, please contact Sintraminercol at sintrami@.telecom.com.co.

Notes

Introduction

1   *Wall Street Journal*, February 11, 1982, June 17, 1982; "Ex-Im Bank clears $375 million loan for coal venture," *Wall Street Journal* August 13, 1982. European banks also contributed heavily to the project. See "Colombia Coal Authority Gets $50 Million Credit," *Wall Street Journal*, January 25, 1982.

2   Gil Klein, "Exxon Mine Project in Colombia Nettles U.S. Coal Community," *Christian Science Monitor*, June 14, 1985.

3   Deborah Pacini Hernandez, "Resource Development and Indigenous People: The El Cerrejón Project in Guajira, Colombia" (Cultural Survival Occasional Paper 15, December 1984), 13.

4   Pacini Hernandez, "Resource Development and Indigenous People," 20-22. The sacred Cerro de la Teta mountain was included in one of the reservas earmarked for construction materials.

5   Remedios Fajardo Gómez, "Violación sistemática de los derechos humanos de indígenas, negros y campesinos por parte de la multinacional minera Intercor, filial de la Exxon, en el departamento de La Guajira, Colombia," ms., August 9, 2001.

6   Pacini Hernandez, "Resource Development and Indigenous People," 27.

7   *Ibid.*, 29, 31.

8   Paraphrased in Al Gedicks, "War on Subsistence: Exxon Minerals/Rio Algomm vs WATER," in Barbara Rose Johnston, *Life and Death Matters: Human Rights and the Environment at the End of the Millennium* (Alta Mira Press, 1997). http://www.menominee.com/nomining/waronxn3.html.

9   Fajardo Gómez, "Violación sistemática de los derechos humanos."

10   Armando Pérez Araujo, et al, "The London Declaration," (released September 2001), http://www.minesandcommunities.org/Charter/londondec.htm. Two other representatives of Yanama are also among the signatories.

Prologue

1   Luis Carlos Restrepo, "La sangre de Gaitán," in *El saqueo de una illusion. El 9 de abril 50 años después* (Bogotá: Número Ediciones, 1997), pp. 179-189. Gaitán was a populist politician who rose to national prominence when he denounced the 1928 massacre of banana workers on a United Fruit Company plantation. His assassination in 1948 unleashed a popular rebellion, and a savage reprisal, setting the stage for the long civil war known as *la violencia* which many analysts see as the direct root of today's violence.

The Profits of Extermination

1   We use the following classifications for miners, although they can vary by region: subsistence miners are indigenous and Afro-Colombians; small miners are small-scale miners, peasants, and squatters; medium miners are small businessmen with some technological infrastructure; large miners are big businesses and multinational companies.

2   See the decision by the Colombian Consejo de Estado (Council of State; Colombia's highest court of administrative law) regarding a dispute between settlers in Santiago de las Atalayas and the State about ownership of subsoil petroleum deposits in the region.

3   See "Urgent Actions" by the José Alvear Restrepo Lawyers'

Collective regarding the Kankuamo community that lives in the Sierra Nevada de Santa Marta, in the north of Colombia, and others like the U'wa in Boyacá.

4   Military aid is the final phase in the implementation of international agreements and legislative changes, which culminated in Plan Colombia. For Richardson's statements in Cartagena, see Kirk Semple, "Energy Officials Mull Colombian Reforms," *Platt's Oilgram News*, April 27, 1999.

5   Statistics from the Contraloría General de la República. For school attendance statistics, see UNICEF, "The State of the World's Children, 2004." Although official figures show up to 90% of Colombia's children having access to primary school (and 70% to secondary school), the rates are much lower among the poor and the displaced.

6   The Spanish companies Endesa, Engesa, and Unión Fenosa have been the most important beneficiaries in the energy sector. Privatization has been accompanied by significant corruption, and preceded by the assassination of several union leaders in the sector, the virtual disappearance of unions, and infiltration by international union bodies that maintain close ties with the multinationals through pension and investment funds.

7   This has occurred in the case of Drummond, the State Bank, and the private television companies Caracol, RCN, and City TV (a Canadian company).

8   See reports by the Cinep and Justicia y Paz database, and the report by the magazine *Noche y Niebla*, put out by the same organization. Colombia's Constitutional Court declared the zones unconstitutional in November of 2002.

9   The Sur American Gold Corporation, through its Colombian subsidiary, Exploradora la Esperanza, has participated in exploration proposals with Corona Goldfields in the

South of Bolívar and some unimportant gold explorations in the Andean zone. According to the Colombian journal *Cromos*, the company, which also owns Grancolombia S.A., announced the discovery of a huge deposit, causing its stock prices to rise. When a state official announced that the deposit did not exist, the stocks fell again. But the company earned several million dollars in the process. See *Cromos* #26, March 31, 1997.

10   Peasants and miners testified about this process at the Forum on Mining, Environment and Peace organized by Sintraminercol, the Canadian embassy, Kairos, and other organizations.

11   Statistics from the Ministry of Mines and the UPME (Unidad de Planeación Minero-Energética; the Mining-Energy Planning Unit of the Ministry of Mines and Energy) for 1996.

12   A *municipio* is somewhat comparable to a county in the United States. Colombia is divided into departments (provinces), and each department is divided into *municipios* which encompass an urban center and the surrounding rural towns.

13   Public document no. 2760, 2 November 1950, which described the sale of these mines.

14   On 11 June 1992 Alfonso López Rodríguez led a commission on a second visit to the area to draw up the boundaries of the Illera family's mines. He concluded that "after traversing the entire area no evidence at all was found of any mining activities carried out on the part of the title-holders requesting recognition of Private Property 026." It is worth noting that both investigations led to the same conclusion.

15   In #2 and #3 on the form, respectively.

16   See Sean Donahue, "The Other Harken Energy Scandal: Oil, Death Squads and Corruption in Colombia," *Counterpunch*,

July 12, 2002; Jeffrey St. Clair and Alexander Cockburn, "Bush's Felonious Friend," *Eat the State!* Vol. 6, #11, January 16, 2002.

17   On March 17, 1995 , the company was legally constituted with a capital of $500 USD. License number 00639965, registered on March 31 1995 under no. 487094, Book 9 of the Bogotá Chamber of Commerce.

18   On March 22, 1995, in the 6th notary in Barranquilla.

19   The Aramburo and Ricaurte Temporary Partnership was formed on July 21, 1995, exclusively to fulfill the contract with the UPME. See Contract No. 153/95, September 20, 1995 between the Temporary Partnership Aramburo and Ricaurte and Fiduciar, under the auspices of the Ministry of Mines.

20   See also articles 7, 34, 35, 36, 37, 38, 98, 99, 100, 101, 102.

21   Proyecto de ley (bill introduced) No. 187/98, House, "For the Reform of the Mining Code."

22   Declarations before the Produraduría and the Fiscalía by public officials of the Alcaldía, detained in the paramilitary operation.

23   Asociación Agrominera del Sur de Bolívar, Agro-Mining Association of the South of Bolívar, today Fedeagromisbol, an organization of 3,500 miners who work in the zone. Asagromisbol has spearheaded the charges and the mobilizations demanding the respect for miners' rights.

24   Bulletin Contents-Conquistador Mines, Ltd., February 8, 2000. In a recent interview, a spokesperson for AngloGold acknowledged that they had actually bought 52% of the shares in Conquistador.

25   Another Canadian company, BMR Gold, withdrew from

some relatively unimportant mining projects it was engaged in because of the conflictive conditions in Colombia.

26 Alleging the "manifest urgency" of the situation, they contracted the Temporary Partnership Martínez Córdoba and Associates through the fiduciary Fiducor S.A. on February 19, 1999, without any public bidding process.

27 Adriana Martínez Villega and Martínez Canabal and Company, S.A. created a Temporary Partnership on January 15, 1999, "because they have been invited to serve as legal consultants to prepare, design, and defend legislation for the reform of the Mining Code." It was not until February 1, 1999 that the UPME made this exclusive offer public.

28 A legal mechanism by which the state, through its agency Minercol Ltda., certifies a mining title.

29 A company belonging to the Holder Bank of Switzerland, part of the Holcim Group and the third largest cement company in the world. Other Colombian cement companies also belong to this group.

30 A company that belongs to the family of former president Andrés Pastrana Arango. His cousins Andrés Uribe Crane, Carlos Andrés Uribe Arango and Ricardo Uribe Arango sit on its board of directors. It was also the second-largest financial donor to Pastrana Arango's presidential campaign.

31 This company belongs to Cemex, and its parent company controls Transportadora Minera y Comercial S.A., Construcciones e Inversiones Diamante Ltda., Jumaji International Corporation, Jupiter Glow Corporation, Excelsior Holdings Investment Inc., Cemex Generación y Comercialización de Energía S.A., Cemex, Transportes de Colombia, etc.

32 See "Memorias de los Foros de Minería, Medio Ambiente y

Paz." Edición de Sintraminercol, 2001.

33 Colombia's 1991 Constitution defines the country as an "estado social de derecho" or "social state of law." This progressive language means that the State is defined as functioning under the rule of law and promoting the political, social, and economic rights of all its citizens. It defines the role of the state in protecting social rights and economic rights more broadly than does traditional liberal thought of the nineteenth century, or neoliberal policy of the late twentieth.

34 Ruling C-339 of 2002.

35 In a letter dated November 29, 1999 to the Director of the UPME, Martínez Córdoba and Associates acknowledge that "Since up to now our meetings with indigenous spokespeople have not had positive results," the responsibility for changing the legislation would be left to Congress, thus disregarding the consultative process mandated by Law 21 of 1991, and expanded by the ILO Convention 169.

36 According to statistics from the Departamento de Planeación Nacional (National Planning Department), cities and departments in the mining regions occupy first place in the National Index of Unsatisfied Needs. They lack basic health services, roads, education, housing, and jobs.

37 Securitization, or *titularización de activos* in Spanish, refers to a process of obtaining a loan based on expected earnings on new investments. The investments are then declared as losses, and are repaid by a state loan guarantee fund, meaning that the citizens are actually paying to finance the paramilitaries.

38 This company operates in an area of 5,111 hectares on private property in the community of Cerrejón. In all, this

operation has been causing losses to the country of US $4 for every ton of coal exported. Prior to its privatization it was exporting 18 million tons per year. The request was made in Brief 3470 presented by company attorney Alfonso Gómez Rengifo and Carbones Colombianos del Cerrejón S.A. on February 5, 2001.

39   Rulings C-863/01, August 15, 2001; C-1049/01 of October 4, 2001 and C-1211/01 of November 21, 2001 determined that the court had already declared Article 5 unconstitutional, and that this decision would be upheld.

40   Statistics from UNICEF. The union's own research indicates that this figure should be doubled.

41   Letter from Julio F. Carbó Artola, commercial attaché at the U.S. Embassy, July 27, 1998. For an updated view, see the U.S. Department of Energy's "An Energy Overview of Colombia," which examines the different energy sectors and applauds the legal changes since the 1990s that have benefited foreign investors. http://www.fe.doe.gov/international/colbover.html.

42   According to the televised newscast "Hora Cero."

43   The report is available at www.nocheyniebla.org.

44   Lawyers of the United Steelworkers of America and the International Labor Rights Fund in the name of Sintramienergética and the families of the workers killed, have brought suit against Drummond before the U.S. District Court in Alabama. See below for further discussion of the case.

45   After the United States, Japan is the largest contributor to Plan Colombia. Japan has established a presence in the zone known as the Mande Batholith—Mutata, Pavarandó, Pavarandocito, and Carmen del Atrato—a

region of continuous paramilitary operations—that contains significant quantities of uranium.

46 Proposed Law no. 201 of 1999.

47 A "state reserve" is an area of land belonging to a state entity for the exploitation of its resources. Under pressure from the World Bank (which wished to see mining production completely privatized), the recent Mining Code abolished these reserves.

48 In 1999 soldiers in Brazilian border battalions confessed that they and the Colombian army had massacred six mineworkers (called Garimpeiros, because they work in the Serranía del Garimpo), with the goal of producing forced displacement. The Normandy and Greenstone companies have made offers to exploit these mines.

49 Coincidentally, a number of military officers who have been accused of leading and continuing to lead paramilitary operations in strategic zones have been trained in the U.S. Army School of the Americas, including Alvaro Hernán Velandia Hurtado, Farouk Yanine Díaz, Hernando Navas Rubio, Carlos Gil Colorado, Rogelio Correa Campos, Harold Bedoya Pizarro and Jesús María Clavijo Clavijo, among others. Taken from report by the International Campaign for Magdalena Medio.

50 See Germán Castro Caycedo, *Con las manos en alto* (Editorial Planeta, 2001).

51 See Jason Vest, "DynCorp's Drug Problem," *The Nation*, July 16, 2001. http://web.archive.org/web/20030720230948/ www.thenation.com/docprint.mhtml?i=20010716&s=vest2 0010703.

52 See the magazine *Semana*, July 2001.

53 See the Guatemalan Truth Commission Report regarding

the role of U.S. advisors in training the death squads in that country.

54 See Human Rights Watch, *Colombia's Killer Networks: The Military-Paramilitary Partnership and the United States*, Part II (New York: Human Rights Watch, 1996); Carlos Medina Gallego and Mireya Téllez Ardila, *La violencia parainstitucional, paramilitar y parapolicial en Colombia* (Santafé de Bogotá: Rodríguez Quito Editores, 1994), pp. 88-89; Amnesty International reports on Colombia for 1982 and 1987. Amnesty has managed to get the U.S. government to declassify the CIA archives which show the collaboration of the CIA with the "Los Pepes" group that was the origin of the ACCU. See also paramilitary leader Carlos Castaño's comments on business support for the paramilitaries in Reuters, "Colombia Paramilitary Chief Says Businesses Back Him," *New York Times*, September 7, 2000. Lawsuits are currently being prepared against companies like Occidental Petroleum, Texaco, Conquistador Mines, and Exxon for their relationships with the paramilitaries.

55 Report by Human Rights Watch, November 1996. http://www.hrw.org/reports/1996/killertoc.htm.

56 Two Bell Ranger 206 helicopters were stolen on November 2, 1999 from Narganá Island. See *La Nación de Panamá*.

57 Noticiero Caracol Televisión, April 2000.

58 Interviews with miners and peasants who were detained by paramilitary commanders and who were later freed. This information was checked with an international human rights defense group that corroborated their testimony. For security reasons, this group asked not to be named. An account of the illicit trail of arms through Nicaragua and Panama to the Colombian paramilitaries, in the hands of Israeli arms

merchants and apparently financed through Plan Colombia, appears in Michelle Lescure, "International Weapons Smuggling Scandal Revealed," *World Press Review*, April 26, 2002.

59   "La operacón buscaba financiar a los paras," interview with Baruch Vega, *El Espectador*, December 1 2002.

60   Up to 42% of the assets of the drug traffickers. *Ibid.*, and "La Revista" section of *El Espectador*, March 23, 2003. See also Jay Weaver, "Feds Tell Why they Dropped Charges Against Drug Informant," *Miami Herald*, Feb. 4, 2003; Tim Johnson, "Did DEA Informants Swindle Drug Lords?" *Miami Herald*, May 21, 2000; "Dr. B and Group 43," *St. Petersburg Times*, May 4, 2003.

61   He is referring to the peace process that was being carried out with the FARC-EP (Fuerzas Armadas Revolucionarias de Colombia-Ejército Popular, Colombia's largest and oldest guerrilla organization), which sought to grant them the status of combatants. *Revista Cambio*, n. 383, October 2000; Juan Forero, "Rightist Squads in Colombia Beating the Rebels," *New York Times,* December 5, 2000.

62   According to statistics from the Comisión Nacional de Regalías (CNR, National Royalties Commission), Córdoba grew in only three years from representing 6.22% of the national total of gold royalties to 60.14% in 1998.

63   A well-known ex-Mayor of a gold-producing *municipio* in the South of Bolívar commented in an interview that the public works were being financed with half of the money that came from the CNR, because they had reached an agreement with the drug traffickers that they would declare the gold that they mined in other *municipios* as originating from the one where he was mayor, and they would split the benefits

50/50. The ex-official explained that this was the only way to obtain money for infrastructure in his *municipio*.

64   See reports by Minga for the years cited.

65   The union leaders repeatedly asked for permission to sleep inside the mine's installations. On several occasions the paramiltiaries had stopped the buses that transported workers from the mine to the city to ask for union leaders.

66   International Labor Rights Fund, "Colombian Union May Proceed Against Drummond Company for the Murder of Union Leaders and for the Violation of its Rights to Associate and Organize," Press Release, April 15, 2003. http://www.laborrights.org/press/drummond041503.htm.

67   The BP oil company in Casanare, Arauca and Antioquia, the Drummond coal company in Cesar and Magdalena, and the banana companies in Urabá and Magdalena have all been criticized in this regard. See, for example, Human Rights Watch, "World Report 1999: Special Programs and Campaigns-Corporations and Human Rights." http://hrw.org/worldreport99/special/corporations.html.

68   See Karl Penhaul, "Americans Blamed in Colombia Attack," *San Francisco Chronicle*, June 15, 2001. See also Human Rights Watch, *The "Sixth Division": Military-Paramilitary Ties and U.S. Policy in Colombia* (New York: Human Rights Watch, 2001), 92-94; T. Christian Miller, "Colombian Air Force Chief Quits," *Los Angeles Times*, August 26, 2003.

69   According to statistics provided by Félix Moreno Posada in the journal *Blanco y negro de las privatizaciones* and from the Contraloría General de la República.

70   Statistics from the Contraloría General de la República.

71   The sale of Carbocol, the state entity that was part owner of the El Cerrejón mine, produced $300 million in losses,

calculated according to reports from the Comptroller's office and independent investigators.

72　The Gini coefficient measures economic inequality. The higher the number (between zero and one), the greater the inequality in resource distribution. Statistics from the Contraloría General de la República at www.contraloriagen. gov.co.

73　Contraloría General de la República, *Colombia: entre la exclusión y el desarrollo. Propuestas para la transición al estado social de derecho*. Percentages calculated by Sintraminercol.

74　*Ibid.*

75　Taken from the study by Censat Agua Viva-Amigos de la Tierra Colombia, "Impactos socioambientales de la minería abierta de carbón: caso del Cerrejón Zona Norte, como muestra tipo de impacto ambiental de gran minería."

76　Cinep and Justicia y Paz database, and statistical research by Sintraminercol and Nomadesc. A massacre is defined as an attack in which four or more people are killed.

77　Calculated from reports by Codhes, Nomadesc and Sintraminercol.

78　Figures from the Sinteraminercol human rights department and the national human rights team of the CUT.

Fig. 1

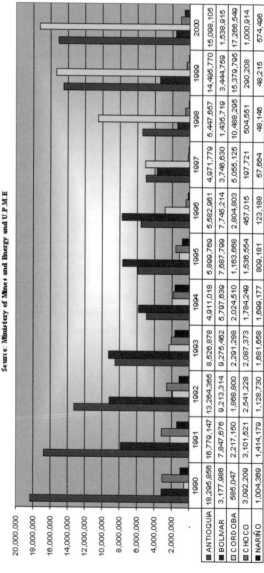

MAIN GOLD-PRODUCING DEPARTMENTS
PRODUCTION IN GRAMS
1990 -2000
Source: Ministery of Mines and Energy and U.P.M.E

	1990	1991	1992	1993	1994	1995	1996	1997	1998	1999	2000
ANTIOQUIA	18,295,856	16,779,147	13,264,365	8,526,878	4,911,018	5,899,769	5,582,961	4,971,779	5,447,657	14,495,770	15,098,105
BOLIVAR	3,177,986	7,847,676	9,213,314	9,275,462	5,797,639	7,687,799	7,745,214	3,746,630	1,435,719	3,444,759	1,538,915
CORDOBA	585,047	2,217,150	1,866,800	2,291,288	2,024,510	1,163,668	2,804,803	5,055,125	10,488,295	15,379,795	17,266,549
CHOCO	3,092,209	3,101,521	2,541,228	2,087,373	1,784,249	1,536,554	467,015	197,721	504,551	290,208	1,000,914
NARIÑO	1,004,369	1,414,179	1,128,730	1,681,658	1,699,177	809,181	123,188	57,664	48,146	48,215	574,496

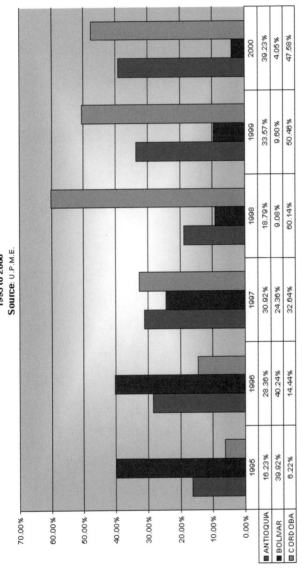

PERCENT OF ROYALTIES RECEIVED BY DIFFERENT DEPARTMENTS
1995 to 2000
Source: U.P.M.E.

	1995	1996	1997	1998	1999	2000
ANTIOQUIA	15.23%	28.36%	30.92%	18.79%	33.57%	39.23%
BOLIVAR	39.92%	40.24%	24.36%	9.08%	9.60%	4.05%
CORDOBA	6.22%	14.44%	32.64%	60.14%	50.46%	47.58%

Fig. 2

Fig. 3

Forced displacement in mining/petroleum *municipios* and non-mining/petroleum *municipios*, 2002

Source: Codhes

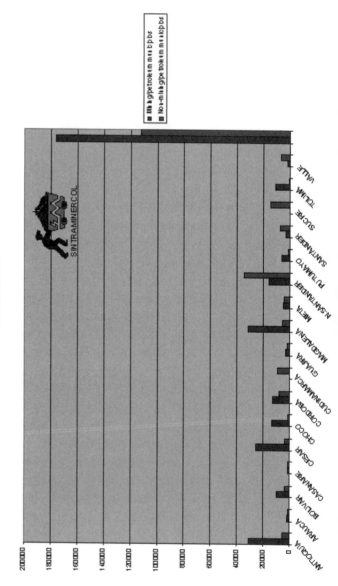

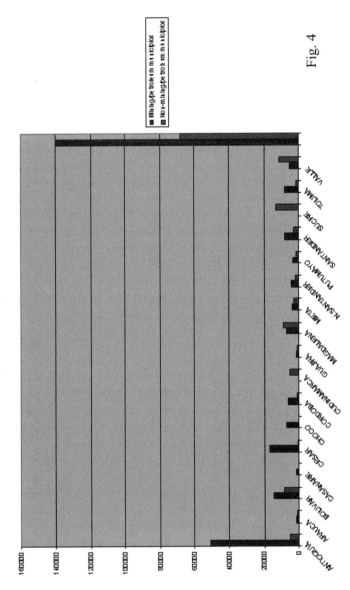

Forced displacement in mining/petroleum *municipios* and non-mining/petroleum *municipios*, 2001

Fig. 4

Fig. 5

Forced displacement in mining-petroleum *municipios* and non-mining-petroleum *municipios*, 2000

Source: Codhes

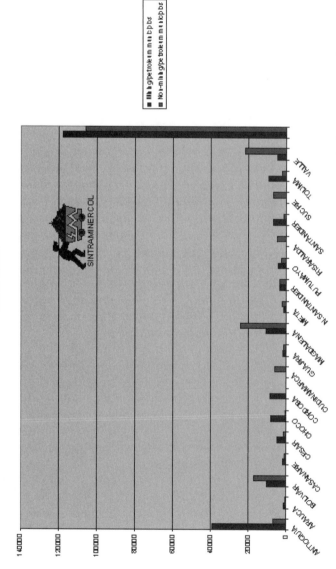

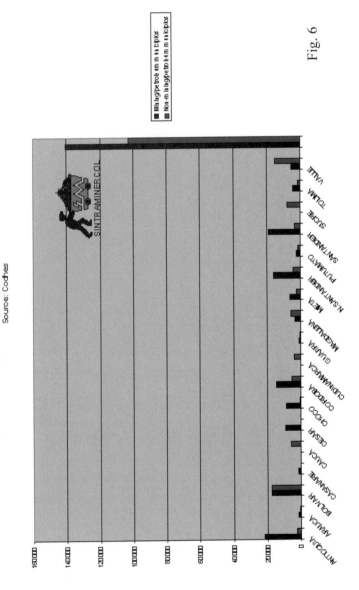

Forced displacement in mining/petroleum *municipios* and non-mining/petroleum *municipios*, 1998
Source: Codhes

Fig. 6

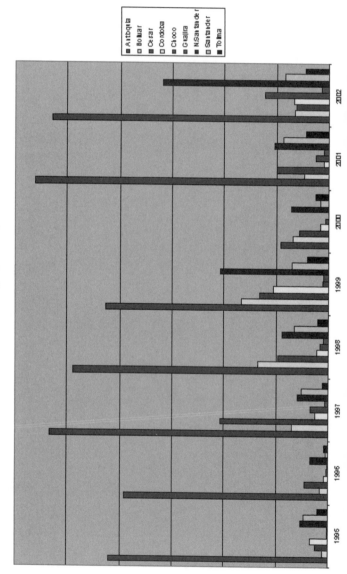

Fig. 7

Total Homicides in Mining Departments, 1995-2002

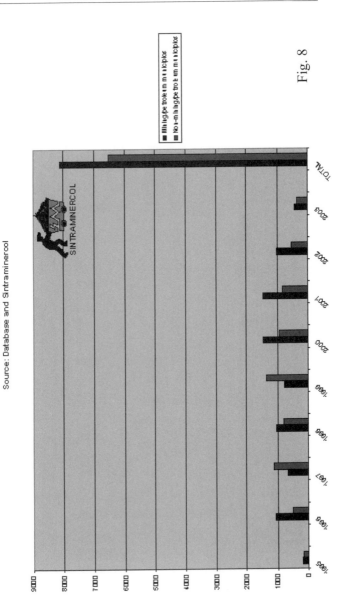

Human rights violations in mining/petroleum *municipios* and non-mining/petroleum *municipios*
1995-2003

Source: Database and Sintraminercol

Fig. 8

Fig. 9

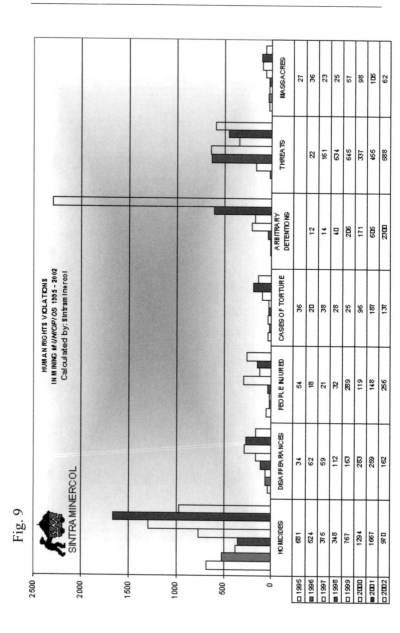

HUMAN RIGHTS VIOLATIONS
IN MINING MUNICIPIOS 1995 - 2002
Calculated by: Sintraminercol

SINTRA MINERCOL

	HOMICIDES	DISAPPEARANCES	PEOPLE INJURED	CASES OF TORTURE	ARBITRARY DETENTIONS	THREATS	MASSACRES
1995	681	34	54	36			27
1996	524	62	18	20	12	22	36
1997	375	59	21	38	14	161	23
1998	348	112	32	28	40	634	25
1999	767	163	289	25	206	645	57
2000	1294	283	119	96	171	337	98
2001	1667	259	148	187	605	455	105
2002	970	162	256	137	2300	588	62

C.C.B.

CAMARA DE COMERCIO DE BOGOTA

CALLE 93

FECHA: DIA 28 MES 02 AÑO 96 HORA 09:54:35

02R160228069   PAGINA: 1
* *

CERTIFICADO DE EXISTENCIA Y REPRESENTACION LEGAL O INSCRIPCION
DE DOCUMENTOS.
LA CAMARA DE COMERCIO DE BOGOTA, CON FUNDAMENTO EN LAS MATRICULAS
E INSCRIPCIONES DEL REGISTRO MERCANTIL,
                        CERTIFICA :

NOMBRE:
COMPAñIA MINERA SAN LUCAS LIMITADA
NIT:***********
DOMICILIO:SANTAFE DE BOGOTA D.C.
                        CERTIFICA :

MATRICULA NO.639965
                        CERTIFICA :
CONSTITUCION: E.P. NO. 893 NOTARIA 36 DE SANTAFE DE BOGOTA DEL 17
DE MARZO DE 1995, INSCRITA EL 31 DE MARZO DE 1995 BAJO EL NUMERO
487094 DEL LIBRO IX, SE CONSTITUYO LA SOCIEDAD COMERCIAL DENOMINA
DA: COMPAñIA MINERA SAN LUCAS LIMITADA
                        CERTIFICA :
VIGENCIA: LA SOCIEDAD NO SE HALLA DISUELTA. DURACION: DEL 17 DE -
MARZO DE 1995 AL 17 DE MARZO DEL AñO 2025
                        CERTIFICA :
OBJETO SOCIAL: PRINCIPAL: LA EXPLORACION, EXPLOTACION, TRANSFORMA
CION, FUNDICION, PROCESAMIENTO, BENEFICIO, TRANSPORTE Y DISTRIBU-
CION DE TODA CLASE DE MINERALES. PARA ELLO PODRA SOLICITAR AL MI-
NISTERIO DE MINAS, MINERALCO S.A., ECOCARBON S.A., O LAS ENTIDA--
DES QUE HAGAN SUS VECES, LICENCIAS, CONTRATOS, APORTES, TAMBIEN -
PODRA REALIZAR CONTRATOS CON PROPIETARIOS DE MINAS, CONTRATOS DE
EXPLORACION, EXPLOTACION, ARRIENDO Y EN GENERAL TODA CLASE DE CON
TRATOS PARA DESARROLLAR EL OBJETO, PODRA COMPRAR, VENDER MINAS Y
DERECHOS MINEROS, ACEPTARLAS EN TRASPASO, CEDERLAS O TRASPASARLAS
TOTAL O PARCIALMENTE, APORTARLAS A COMPAñIAS Y EMPRESA QUE PARA -
ELLO SE ORGANICEN, CELEBRAR TODA CLASE DE CONTRATOS Y EJECUTAR --
LOS ACTOS CIVILES Y COMERCIALES QUE SEAN NECESARIAS PARA EL LOGRO
DE ESTOS PROPOSITOS, PODRA REPRESENTAR FIRMAS NACIONALES O EXTRAN
JERAS QUE SE DEDIQUEN A CUALQUIER ACTIVIDAD DE TIPO MINERO. LA AD
QUISICION Y COMERCIALIZACION DE BIENES PARA EMPRESAS MINERAS, LA
COMPRAVENTA DE MAQUINARIA, VEHICULOS Y EQUIPOS DESTINADOS A LOS -
FINES DE LA EMPRESA, IMPORTACION Y EXPORTACION DE PRODUCTOS NECE-
SARIOS A LA REALIZACION DE LAS DISTINTAS ACTIVIDADES MINERAS, EN
DESARROLLO DE SU OBJETO SOCIAL, LA COMERCIALIZACION DE BIENES MUE
BLES E INMUEBLES EN DESARROLLO DE SU OBJETO SOCIAL, LA FACULTAD -
DE HACERSE PARTE EN OTRAS EMPRESAS QUE TENGAN IGUALES O SIMILARES
ACTIVADES. EN DESARROLLO DE SU OBJETO SOCIAL LA SOCIEDAD PODRA: -
A.- CELEBRAR CONTRATO DE MANDATO CIVIL Y COMERCIAL. - B- ADQUIRIR
ENAJENAR, PERMUTAR, GRAVAR, TOMAR Y DAR EN ARRENDAMIENTO TODA CLA
SE DE BIENES MUEBLES E INMUEBLES. - C.- INTERVENIR ANTE TERCEROS
COMO DEUDORA O ACREEDORA DE TODA CLASE DE OPERACIONES DE CREDITO,
DANDO O RECIBIENDO GARANTIAS CUANDO HAYA LUGAR. - D.- CELEBRAR --
CON ESTABLECIMIENTO DE CREDITO Y COMPAñIAS ASEGURADORAS TODA CLA-

Document 1. Certificate of existence and legal representation of the Compañía
Minera San Lucas.

C.C.B. `* 0 1 *   7 4 0 6 3 7 *`

CAMARA DE COMERCIO DE BOGOTA

CALLE 93

FECHA: DIA 28 MES 02 AÑO 96 HORA 09:54:44

02R160228069   PAGINA: 2
* *

SE DE OPERACIONES DE CREDITO Y DE SEGURO QUE SE RELACIONEN CON --
LOS NEGOCIOS Y BIENES SOCIALES. - E.- GIRAR, ACEPTAR, ENDOSAR, --
ASEGURAR, COBRAR, PIGNORAR, CEDER Y NEGOCIAR EN GENERAL TITULOS -
VALORES CUALESQUIERA OTRA CLASE DE TITULOS DE CREDITO. ---- F.---
FORMAR PARTE DE OTRAS SOCIEDADES QUE SE PROPONGAN ACTIVIDADES SE-
MEJANTES, COMPLEMENTARIAS O ACCESORIAS DE LA EMPRESA SOCIAL, O --
PERMITIR QUE OTRAS SOCIEDADES FORMEN PARTE DE ESTA SOCIEDAD,TRANS
FORMARSE EN OTRO TIPO DE SOCIEDAD O FUSIONARSE CON OTRA U OTRAS -
SOCIEDADES. - G.- CELEBRAR Y EJECUTAR EN GENERAL TODOS LOS ACTOS
O CONTRATOS PREPARATORIOS, COMPLEMENTARIOS O ACCESORIOS DE TODOS
LOS ANTERIORES, LO QUE SE RELACIONEN CON LA EXISTENCIA Y FUNCIONA
MIENTO DE LA SOCIEDAD Y LOS DEMAS QUE SEAN CONDUCENTES AL LOGRO -
DE LOS FINES SOCIALES.-
                        CERTIFICA :
CAPITAL Y SOCIOS: $1.000.000.00 DIVIDIDO EN 100 CUOTAS DE VALOR -
NOMINAL DE $100.000.00 CADA UNA, DISTRIBUIDO ASI:
SOCIOS   DOCUMENTO IDENTF.   NO. CUOTAS   VALOR
LUISA FERNANDA
ARAMBURO RESTREPO   C.C.41.793.395   50 $500.000.00
JAMES DAVID
GREENBAUM   PASP. NO. 032077539   50   500.000.00
                                             ---   ------------
TOTALES: 100 $1.000.000.00
                        CERTIFICA :
REPRESENTACION LEGAL. EL REPRESENTANTE LEGAL ES EL GERENTE Y SU
SUPLENTE O SUBGERENTE
                        CERTIFICA :
POR ESCRITURA DE CONSTITUCION CITADA, FUERON NOMBRADOS:
CARGO   NOMBRE   DOC. IDENTF.
GERENTE: JAMES D. GREENBAUM   PASP. NO. 032077539
SUPLENTE O
SUBGERENTE: LUISA FERNANDA ARAMBURO RESTREPO C.C.41.793.395
                        CERTIFICA :
FACULTADES DEL REPRESENTANTE LEGAL: LA SOCIEDAD TENDRA UN GERENTE
Y UN SUPLENTE O SUBGERENTE QUE LO REEMPLAZARA EN SUS FALTAS ABSO-
LUTAS, TEMPORALES O ACCIDENTALES Y CUYA DESIGNACION Y REMOCION DE
PENDERA TAMBIEN DE LA JUNTA. EL GERENTE Y EL SUBGERENTE TENDRAN -
UN PERIODO DE UN AÑO, SIN PERJUICIO DE QUE PUEDAN SER REELEGIDOS
INDEFINIDAMENTE O REMOVIDOS EN CUALQUIER TIEMPO. EL GERENTE ES EL
REPRESENTANTE LEGAL DE LA SOCIEDAD, CON FACULTADES PARA EJECUTAR
TODOS LOS ACTOS Y CONTRATOS ACORDES CON LA NATURALEZA DE SU ENCAR
GO Y QUE SE RELACIONEN DIRECTAMENTE CON EL GIRO ORDINARIO DE LOS
NEGOCIOS SOCIALES. EN ESPECIAL TENDRA LAS SIGUIENTES FUNCIONES: -
A.- DESIGNAR LOS EMPLEADOS QUE REQUIERA EL NORMAL FUNCIONAMIENTO
DE LA COMPAñIA Y SEñALARLES SU REMUNERACION, EXCEPTO QUE POR LEY
O LOS ESTATUTOS DEBAN SER DESIGNADOS POR LA JUNTA GENERAL DE SO--
CIOS. - B.- PRESENTAR UN INFORME DE SU GESTION A LA JUNTA GENERAL
DE SOCIOS EN SUS REUNIONES ORDINARIAS Y EL BALANCE DE FIN DE EJER

Document 2. Certificate of existence and legal representation of the Compañía Minera San Lucas, p.2.

C.C.B.

CAMARA DE COMERCIO DE BOGOTA

CALLE 93

FECHA: DIA 28 MES 02 AÑO 96 HORA 09:54:51

02R160228069   PAGINA: 3

CICIO CON UN PROYECTO DE DISTRIBUCION DE UTILIDADES. - C.- CONVO-
CAR LA JUNTA GENERAL DE SOCIOS A REUNIONES ORDINARIAS Y EXTRAORDI
NARIAS. - D.- NOMBRAR LOS ARBITROS QUE CORRESPONDAN A LA SOCIEDAD
EN VIRTUD DE COMPROMISOS, CUANDO ASI LO AUTORICE LA JUNTA GENERAL
DE SOCIOS, Y DE LA CLAUSULA COMPROMISORIA QUE EN ESTOS ESTATUTOS
SE PACTA. -E.- CONSTITUIR APODERADOS JUDICIALES Y EXTRAJUDICIALES
CON FACULTADES EXPRESAS,PARA LA DEFENSA DE LOS INTERESES SOCIALES
F.- CELEBRAR TODA CLASE DE CONTRATOS QUE SE REQUIERAN PARA EL DE-
SARROLLLO DEL OBJETO SOCIAL HASTA EL LIMITE DE DOSCIENTOS MILLO--
NES DE PESOS ($200.000.000). EN CASO DE QUE EL CONTRATO SOBREPASE
ESTA SUMA REQUERIRA APROBACION DE LA JUNTA GENERAL DE SOCIOS.-
                    CERTIFICA :
DIRECCION DE NOTIFICACION JUDICIAL:
CL. 99 NO. 9A-54 (202)
MUNICIPIO: SANTAFE DE BOGOTA D.C.
                    CERTIFICA :
QUE NO FIGURAN INSCRIPCIONES ANTERIORES A LA FECHA DEL PRESENTE
CERTIFICADO, QUE MODIFIQUEN TOTAL O PARCIALMENTE SU CONTENIDO.

SANTA FE DE BOGOTA, D.C. FECHA: DIA 28 MES 02 AÑO 96

EL SECRETARIO DE LA CAMARA DE COMERCIO DE BOGOTA,

VALOR : $ 1360

            NO CAUSA IMPUESTO DE TIMBRE

Document 3. Certificate of existence and legal representation of the Compañía Minera San Lucas, p.3.

REPUBLICA DE COLOMBIA

MINISTERIO DE MINAS Y ENERGIA

Jun 11 8 cu AM '92
011288
DEPENDENCIA
NUMERO :

VISITA DE RECONOCIMIENTO DE PROPIEDAD PRIVADA No. 026

Por resoluciones No.3-0407 del 24 de marzo y 3-0535 del 14 de abril del presente año, me desplacé a la jurisdicción de los municipios de Simití y Santa Rosa del Sur, ubicados en el Sur de Bolívar y más exactamente en la Serranía de San Lucas, con el propósito de "Ubicar los rumbos y distancias de todas las minas que se encuentran dentro del Reconocimiento de Propiedad No.026 y observar que trabajos se adelantan en la actualidad".

A continuación me permito transcribir los resultados de dicha visita, la cual se adelantó en compañía del topógrafo de la Sección Regional Minera de Bucaramanga el señor Efraín Camargo Buitrago y del conductor Jorge Elías Amaya.

1.   GENERALIDADES

El área objeto de la visita se encuentra ubicada en la Serranía de San Lucas, la cual presenta los siguientes rasgos fisiográficos:

-   Máxima altura: 1800 m. a 1850 m.s.n.m.
    Punto denominado la "Teta de San Lucas"

Document 4. Report by the Ministry of Mines and Energy on visit to the mines supposedly belonging to the Illera Palacio family.

REPUBLICA DE COLOMBIA

MINISTERIO DE MINAS Y ENERGIA

DEPENDENCIA 61
NUMERO : 4

El sector se encuentra dividido en tres minas esencialmente:

- Mina Nueva
- Mina Vieja
- Mina San Luquitas

Aparte de ellas tiene: mina Fácil, mina Mocho, mina Mosquito, etc.; un asentamiento bastante importante se está formando en el sitio denominado mina Unión, el cual queda a tres horas de camino aprôximadamente de mina Nueva.

4.   CONCLUSIONES Y RECOMENDACIONES

   4.1 Conclusiones
      - "Una vez recorrida toda el <u>área no se encontró evidencia</u> alguna de actividades mineras realizadas por parte de los titulares del Reconocimiento de propiedad privada número 026".

      - En virtud a lo anterior no se hizo necesario ubicar mediante rumbos y distancias ninguna mina de los titulares por ausencia de las mismas.

   4.2 Recomendaciones
      - Dar aplicación a las normas legales que para estos casos se estimen convenientes.

MINISTERIO DE MINAS Y ENERGIA
DIRECCION GENERAL DE MINAS
DIVISION LEGAL DE MINAS,
SECREIARIA LEGAL
A U T E N T I C A C I O·N
Es copia del documento que tuve a la vista
3 MAR. 1997

Document 5. Report by the Ministry of Mines and Energy on visit to the mines supposedly belonging to the Illera Palacio family, p.2.

REPUBLICA DE COLOMBIA

MINISTERIO DE MINAS Y ENERGIA

DEPENDENCIA   61
NUMERO :   5

Legalizar las áreas mineras ocupadas por los mineros
en el Sector central de la Serranía de San Lucas, co-
laborarles mediante un programa de Asistencia Técnica
y Social.

ALFONSO LOPEZ RODRIGUEZ
Ing. en Minas MP 15218 – 18573
División de Asistencia Tecnica
y Fomento Minero.

MINISTERIO DE MINAS Y ENERGIA
DIRECCION GENERAL DE MINAS
DIVISION LEGAL DE MINAS
SECRETARIA LEGAL
A U T E N T I C A C I O N
Es copia del documento que tuvo a la vista
3 MAR. 1997

Document 6. Report by the Ministry of Mines and Energy on visit to the
mines supposedly belonging to the Illera Palacio family, p.3.

0 3 1 0 4 2

Señor
MINISTRO DE MINAS Y ENERGIA
E.   S.   D.

Feb ⟨ ⟩ 81 PM '95

REFERENCIA: RECONOCIMIENTO DE PROPIEDAD PRIVADA No.026.

EFRAIN ILLERA PALACIO, JUAN ILLERA PALACIO, MARIA PAULINA ILLERA
PALACIO, ISABEL ILLERA DE CASTRO Y LEONOR ILLERA DE VISBAL,
mayores y vecinos de Barranquilla, identificados como aparece al
pie de nuestras firmas, de manera atenta me dirijo a Ud. con el
fin de otorgar poder especial amplio y suficiente a la doctora
LUISA FERNANDA ARAMBURO, abogada titulada con T.P. No. 24011 de
M.J., con el fin de que nos representa en el reconocimiento de
propiedad privada de la referencia.

La doctora ARAMBURO queda facultada para recibir, interponer
recursos, sustituir, reasumir este poder y en general adelantar
todas las diligencias necesarias a la defensa de nuestros
intereses.

Señor Ministro,

EFRAIN ILLERA PALACIO
C.C. No. 16.396 de Bogotá

MARIA PAULINA ILLERA PALACIO
C.C. No. 22.251.787 de Barranquilla

LEONOR ILLERA DE VISBAL
C.C. No. 22.251.775 de Barranquilla

Acepto,

LUISA FERNANDA ARAMBURO
C.C. 41.793.395 de Bogotá.
T.P. 24011 de M J

JUAN ILLERA PALACIO
C.C. No. 833.411 de Barranquilla

ISABEL ILLERA de DECASTRO
C.C. No. 22.251.773 de Barranquilla
2 2 2 5 1 7 7 3 - 13 11a

MINISTERIO DE MINAS Y ENERGIA
DIRECCION GENERAL DE MINAS
DIVISION LEGAL DE MINAS
SECRETARIA LEGAL
A U T E N T I C A C I O N
Es copia del documento que tuve a la vista
3 MAR. 1997

Document 7. Letter from the Illera Palacio family granting power of attorney
ot Luisa Fernanda Aramburo.

Entre los suscritos a saber , **EFRAIN ILLERA PALACIO** mayor y vecino de Barranquilla, identificado con la Cédula de Ciudadanía número 16.396 de Bogotá, quien obra en nombre y representación de sus hermanos, de acuerdo al poder que se anexa a este contrato, **JUAN ILLERA PALACIO, MARIA PAULINA ILLERA PALACIO, ISABEL ILLERA DE DE CASTRO Y LEONOR ILLERA DE VISBAL,** quien para los efectos de este contrato se llamará **EL CONTRATANTE** , y **JAMES D. GREENBAUM,** mayor y vecino de Las Vegas, Estados Unidos, identificado con pasaporte número 032077539 de Estados Unidos, quien actua en representación de la sociedad **COMPAÑIA MINERA SAN LUCAS LTDA,** quien para los efectos de este contrato se llamará **LA CONTRATISTA** , han convenido en celebrar el siguiente contrato que se establece en las siguientes cláusulas:

CLAUSULA PRIMERA. - **AREA**- **EL CONTRATANTE** es titular de un reconocimiento de propiedad privada, radicado en el Ministerio de Minas y Energía bajo el número 026, y que para los efectos de éste contrato se llamará **R.P.P. O26.**

CLAUSULA SEGUNDA.- OBJETO DE ESTE CONTRTATO.- En virtud del título anteriormente descrito, **EL CONTRATANTE** se compromete con **LA CONTRATISTA** a permitirle la exploración en la totalidad del área objeto del **R.P.P.026,** dentro de lo cual se incluye , muestreos, análisis, estudios, visitas ocasionales y permanentes, fotografía y aerofotografía, y en general todo tipo de estudios geológicos, geograficos, sociales, etc., en el área objeto del **R.P.P.026** con el fin de establecer la existencia de minerales económicamente explotables, y especialmente la existencia de oro económicamente explotable.

CLAUSULA TERCERA.- EXCLUSIVIDAD PARA LA EXPLOTACION.- Si después de hacer los estudios de exploración descritos en la cláusula anterior, **LA CONTRATISTA** determina la existencia de minerales económicamente explotables tendrá el derecho exclusivo para adelantar la explotación en la totalidad del área distinguida como **R.P.P. O26** , o en el área que **LA CONTRATISTA** escoja y determine.

PARAGRAFO PRIMERO.- Al finalizar los estudios de exploración, **LA CONTRATISTA** entregará una copia completa de los mismos a **EL CONTRATANTE,** en especial los estudios geológicos, geográficos, planos y fotogrfías, así como información de las sumas de dinero invertidas en el proyecto.

PARAGRAFO SEGUNDO.- En el evento en que **LA CONTRATISTA** no este interesada en la totalidad del área del **R.P.P. 026, EL CONTRATANTE** podrá, en el área restante contratar la exploración y explotación con otras personas naturales o jurídicas, o explotar directamente de acuerdo a las área escojidas por **LA CONTRATISTA.**

CLAUSULA CUARTA.- PAGOS, REGALIAS Y PARTICIPACION, LA CONTRATISTA pagará a **EL CONTRATANTE** la suma de **DIEZ MIL DOLARES** (U.S. 10.000) a la firma de éste contrato. En el evento en que **LA CONTRATISTA** decida hacer la explotación pagará a **EL CONTRATANTE** la suma de **VEINTICINCO MIL DOLARES** adicional a los **DIEZ MIL DOLARES** inicialmente pagados.

PARAGRAFO PRIMERO.- Las sumas a que se refiere la Cláusula Cuarta se pagarán en pesos Colombianos, a la tasa de cambio oficial vigente a la fecha de pago, con cheque de gerencia sobre un banco de la ciudad de Barranquilla.

Document 8. Exclusive exploitation contract for the gold deposits claimed by the Illera Palacio family and the Minera San Lucas company.

PARAGRAFO SEGUNDO.- Adicionalmente a las sumas anteriormente descritas, en el evento en que decida explotar el área del **R.P.P. 026**, **LA CONTRATISTA** pagará a **EL CONTRATANTE** por concepto de regalia, lo correspondiente al **CUATRO POR CIENTO (4%)** del mineral neto sacado, después de fundido, de acuerdo al parámetro conocido internacionalmente como NSR (Net Smelter Réturn), y el **UNO POR CIENTO (1%)** de participación en la compañía explotadora.

CLÁUSULA QUINTA.- SISTEMA DE CONTROL Y AUDITORIA.- LA CONTRATISTA Y EL CONTRATANTE establecerán de común acuerdo el sistema de control y auditoría de la producción para determinar el N.S.R. (Net Smelter Return) del cual se calcula el **4%** del las regalías, y el análisis del los Balances y Estados Financieros de la compañía explotadora (Compañía Minera de San Lucas Ltda.) para determinae el 1% de la participación. Este acuerdo deberá estar establecido antes de dar comienzo formal a la explotación.

CLAUSULA SEXTA.- OBLIGACIONES DEL CONTRATANTE.-

a) Permitirle a **LA CONTRATISTA** la exclusiva exploración y posterior explotación en el área objeto del **R.P.P. 026.**

b) Conservar vigente el **R.P.P. 026**, para ello deberá adelantar todas las diligencias necesaria a la protección del título minero.

c) Respetar el derecho de exclusividad de **LA CONTRATISTA** durante el periodo (exploración y explotación, por tanto no podrá realizar contrato alguno con persona natural o jurídica distinta, en el área del **R.P.P. 026**, salvo que **LA CONTRATISTA** manifieste que no tiene ningún interés en realizar trabajos de explotación en el área del **R.P.P.026** , o que manifieste su interés sobre un área especifica, determinada por **LA CONTRATISTA** , caso en el cual **EL CONTRATANTE** podrá realizar contrato con otras personas.

PARAGRAFO.- La violación por parte de **EL CONTRATANTE** de cualquiera de las obligaciones de este contrato dará lugar a la terminación del contrato con indemnización de perjuicios.

CLAUSULA SEPTIMA.- OBLIGACIONES DE LA CONTRATISTA.-

a) Realizar los trabajos de exploración y explotación en forma técnica con el fin de que logre la recuperación ambiental, y en general adoptar y mantener todas las medidas indispensables para evitar, en la medida de lo posible, daños y contaminaciones personas, bienes y recursos.

b) Responder ante terceros por los daños causados con motivo o por causa de la ejecución de este contrato.

c) Atender los requerimientos que presenten las autoridades nacionales, departamentales, municipales, o de cualquier orden, dentro del ámbito de su competencia. Durante la vigencia del presente contrato cumplirá las leyes de Colombia y pagará a cargo de la totalidad de los impuestos que a favor de la Nación, Departamento y Municipio graven el área del **R.P.P.026**, en desarrollo de los trabajos iniciales de exploración y posterior explotación si **LA CONTRATISTA** decide explotar.

PARAGRAFO.- La violación por parte de **LA CONTRATISTA** de cualquiera de las obligaciones de este contrato dará lugar a la terminación del contrato con indemnización de perjuicios.

Document 9. Exclusive exploitation contract for the gold deposits claimed by the Illera Palacio family and the Minera San Lucas company, p.2.

CLAUSULA OCTAVA.- DURACION.- El presente contrato tiene un vigencia de un año, contado a partir de la firma de este convenio. Si transcurrido un año, LA CONTRATISTA decide que el yacimiento objeto del R.P.P.026 es económicamente explotable, EL CONTRATANTE garantiza que el periodo de explotación a favor de LA CONTRATISTA será de veinticinco de VEINTICINDO (25) años.

CLAUSULA NOVENA.- COSTOS.-. Todos los costos de la exploración inicial, y posterior explotación, al igual que los suministros, servicios, mano de obra, impuestos, tasas, regalías y demás contribuciones serán a cargo de LA CONTRATISTA.

CLAUSULA DECIMA.- CLAUSULA COMPROMISORIA . Cualquier diferencia entre CONTRATANTE y CONTRATISTA será sometida a decisión arbitral, por razón de incumplimiento, aplicación, desarrollo e interpretación del presente contrato, durante su ejecución o su expiración. Al efecto las partes conjuntamente nombrarán, según consideren conveniente, bien un sólo árbitro que defina la contraoversia, o tres árbitros que integren el tribunal. Si no hubiere acuerdo para la designación del arbitro único o de los tres árbitros, lo decidirá la Cámara de Comercio de Bogotá.

CLAUSULA DECIMO PRIMERA.- DOMICILIO.- Las partes designan la ciudad de Bogotá como domicilio contractual para todos los efectos legales.

CLAUSULA DECIMO SEGUNDA.- '-En el caso que LA CONTRATISTA decida explotar se lo hará saber por escrito a EL CONTRATANTE dentro del mes siguiente al vencimiento de este contrato, caso en el cual se suscribirá un contrato para la explotación de la totalidad del área del R.P.P.026, o del área que LA CONTRATISTA defina, bajo los mismos parametros en cuanto a la regalía del 4% N.SR., a la participación del 1% en la compañia y a la duración de veinticinco años (25) , auditoria y control , y se someterá, de acuerdo al artículo 22 del Código de Minas, a la aprobación y registro por parte del Ministerio de Minas y Energia.

PARAGRAFO.- En caso que LA CONTRATISTA defina si el área es económicamente explotable o no, podrá avisarle a EL CONTRATANTE en un término inferior al escrito en la cláusula octava de este contrato, caso en el cual suscribirán el contrato de explotación, o quedará el área del R.P.P. 026 libre para cualquier negociación por parte de EL CONTRATANTE.

CLAUSULA DECIMO TERCERA.- PENA y/o POLIZA.- LA CONTRATISTA se obliga a pagar como pena, en caso de incumplimiento de sus obligaciones contractuales la suma de VEINTICINCO MIL DOLARES (25.000) , o de ser posible, y de manera preferencial, a constituir una póliza por valor de VEINTICINCO MIL DOLARES (25.000) o su equivalente en pesos Colombianos a la tasa del cambio oficial, y vigente por la duración del contrato y un mes más.

CLAUSULA DECIMO CUARTA.- ANEXOS.- Son documentos del contrato y por tanto forman parte integral del mismo: a) El certificado de Existencia y Representación legal de la sociedad COMPAÑIA MINERA SAN LUCAS LTDA., expedido por la Cámara de Comercio de Bogotá. b) El poder presentado por el señor EFRAIN ILLERA PALACIO. c)Copia de la certificación expedida por el Ministerio de Minas y Energia en donde acredita que el R.P.P.026 esta vigente.

Document 10. Exclusive exploitation contract for the gold deposits claimed by the Illera Palacio family and the Minera San Lucas company, p.3.

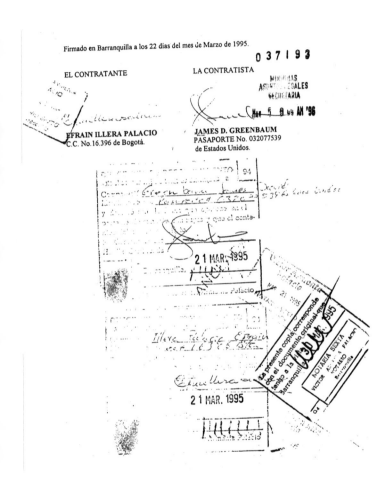

Firmado en Barranquilla a los 22 días del mes de Marzo de 1995.

0 37 1 9 3

EL CONTRATANTE

LA CONTRATISTA

EFRAIN ILLERA PALACIO
C.C. No.16.396 de Bogotá.

JAMES D. GREENBAUM
PASAPORTE No. 032077539
de Estados Unidos.

Document 11. Exclusive exploitation contract for gold deposits claimed by the Illera Palacio family and the Minera San Lucas company, p. 4.

REPUBLICA DE COLOMBIA
MINISTERIO DE MINAS Y ENERGIA

Proyecto Código de Minas

CAPITULO IV

Procedimiento para Suscripción de Contratos de Concesión de Exploración y Explotación

ARTICULO 24. Solicitud de concesión de exploración y explotación. La solicitud de concesión de exploración y explotación se presentará ante la autoridad minera en formularios simplificados y deberá acompañarse de la localización y delimitación técnica del área que se pretende explorar y explotar.

ARTICULO 25. Area de la concesión. El área de la concesión no podrá exceder de treinta mil (30.000) hectáreas y deberá estar determinada por un polígono, amarrado a un punto arcifinio y localizada con los sistemas, procedimientos y medios de carácter técnico que señale el reglamento. Dicha área se considera otorgada por linderos y en consecuencia, el concesionario no tendrá derecho a reclamo alguno en el caso de que la extensión real contenida por tales linderos resultare inferior a la mencionada en el acto de otorgamiento de la concesión.

En el caso de los materiales de construcción el área a que se refiere el inciso anterior no podrá exceder de mil (1000) hectáreas.

ARTICULO 26. Deficiencias en la solicitud. En el término de treinta (30) días, contados desde su presentación, la autoridad minera señalará las deficiencias y omisiones de que adolezcan la solicitud o sus documentos anexos, y si fueren tales que no puedan corregirse oficiosamente e impidan la identificación del interesado, o la comprobación de su representación o ordenará subsanarlas dentro del término que fije para el efecto, so pena de declarar desistida dicha solicitud.

Con todo si la solicitud no permite identificar la localización del área pedida, se tendrá por no presentada.

ARTICULO 27. Criterio para la escogencia entre varios solicitantes. En caso de que se presenten varias solicitudes para una misma área prevalece la que primero se hubiere presentado ante la autoridad competente.

ARTICULO 28. Superposición de áreas. La autoridad minera, dentro del mismo término de treinta (30) días, eliminará de oficio las superposiciones parciales de la solicitud con:

a) Solicitudes anteriores o títulos vigentes, siempre que se refieran a los mismos minerales.

b) Zonas restringidas de que trata el artículo 7 del presente Código, y

Document 12. Text of Article 27 of the 1996 Mining Code proposal approved by the Colombian House of Representatives, which took the mines from the small miners in the South of Bolívar.

THE COMPANY

Conquistador Mines Ltd. is a public company traded on the Vancouver Stock Exchange (Symbol CMG). The Company's purpose is to provide the foundation for and achievement of substantial shareholder value through discovery, acquisition, exploration, and development of large bulk mineable gold and silver deposits.

Conquistador Mines, through its Subsidiary, Corona Goldfields S.A. is engaged in the business of exploring and developing mineral resource properties exclusively in Colombia. The Company's exploration activities are focused on gold and silver. The Company holds numerous granted licenses on various properties in the States of Antioquia and Caldas, Colombia. The Company also has the right to acquire interests in certain exploration and exploitation licenses and/or applications for exploration and exploitation licenses on additional properties located in Colombia.

In addition, the Company has the right to acquire a 50.1% equity interest in Mineros Nacionales S.A., a Colombian public corporation which owns a mining property known as the Marmato Property, located in Caldas State. The Company presently owns 13.15% of the issued and outstanding share capital of Mineros Nacionales S.A.

The host country, Colombia, is rich in natural resources and has one of the most stable economies in the region. Most of the controls on currency exchange and foreign investment have been removed, and taxes have been reduced for foreign investors. Many institutions in Europe rate Colombia in the top three in South America in terms of "Business Risk".

Conquistador is fortunate to be among the first to conduct a modern exploration program in Colombia. Conquistador's primary objective is to significantly increase shareholder value over the next several years. The principal means by which we expect to accomplish this objective will be through the company's expertise in the geology of gold systems and exploration for bulk mineable gold deposits in Colombia.

Document 13. Report by Conquistador mines that shows its relationship with its subsidiary Corona Goldfields, represented by Luisa Fernanda Aramburo.

Bulletins Contents

Bulletin Contents | Unlimited Usage

Conquistador Mines Ltd.
Listed Company

CMG 0.19

CONQUISTADOR MINES LTD. ("CMG")
BULLETIN TYPE: Property-Asset Disposition
BULLETIN DATE: February 8, 2000

CDNX has accepted for filing an option agreement dated November 5, 1999, whereby AngloGold South America Ltd. may acquire up to a 50% interest in the Colombian properties of Conquistador Mines Ltd. exclusive of the Marmato project, by funding US$2,500,000 on the properties within 5 years. AngloGold must fund US$250,000 within the initial 6 month period, US$500,000 within the subsequent 12 month period, and the remaining US$1,750,000 within the following 42 months.

Document 14. Record of stock sales transferring 50% ownership of Conquistador Mines to AngloGold.

Embassy of the United States of America

Santafé de Bogotá, Colombia
Julio 27 de 1998

Doctor
Alfonso Saade
Gerente General (e)
Minerales de Colombia (MINERALCO)
Calle 32 No. 13 - 07
Santa Fé de Bogotá

Estimado Dr. Saade:

La Sección Comercial de la Embajada Americana está preparando un estudio sobre el sector minero de Colombia. En vista del potencial del país en cuanto a depósitos de minerales, y al interés del gobierno colombiano en atraer la inversión extranjera en este sector, le solicitamos información que nos permita preparar monografías de los diferentes minerales, así como un listado de empresas que actualmente están desarrollando operaciones mineras en Colombia.

Esta información ayudará a orientar a empresas americanas y en la promoción de misiones de empresarios colombianos a feria del sector en Estados Unidos. Cualquier información que puedan enviarnos será apreciada. En caso de requerir alguna información de nuestra parte, por favor no dude en comunicarse con nosotros.

Cordialmente

Julio F. Carbó Arrola
Especialista Comercial

 Tel: (571) 315-0811
Ext. 2519 & 2781
Tels. Directas: 315-2126 & 315-2298

Mail From U.S.A.:
USA&FCS
Unit # 5120

Servicio Comercial
Embajada de los Estados Unidos de América
Calle 22 D Bis # 47-51

Document 15. Letter from the U.S. Embassy to Minercol expressing U.S. government interest in Colombian mining.

MARTINEZ CORDOBA & ASOCIADOS

ACUERDO DE UNION TEMPORAL

Los suscritos a saber, ADRIANA MARTINEZ VILLEGAS, mayor y vecina de Santa Fe de Bogotá, D.C., portadora de la cédula de ciudadanía No. 39.693.130 de Usaquén, en representación de MARTINEZ CANABAL Y CIA. S.A., sociedad comercial domiciliada en Santa Fe de Bogotá, con matrícula mercantil No. 00055753 de la Cámara de Comercio de Bogotá, por una parte y por la otra JOSE MARIA CORDOBA PEREZ, mayor y vecino de Santa Fe de Bogotá, identificado con la cédula de ciudadanía No. 2.943.027 de Bogotá, en representación de CORDOBA CARDONA ASOCIADOS LTDA., sociedad comercial domiciliada en Bogotá, con matrícula mercantil No. 222611 de la Cámara de Comercio de Bogotá, considerando que la Unidad de Planeación Minero-Energética del Ministerio de Minas y Energía-UPME, les ha formulado sendas invitaciones para ofrecer sus servicios de asesoría jurídica cuya finalidad es preparar, redactar y sustentar un Proyecto de Ley sobre Reforma del Código de Minas, han resuelto constituír una **Unión Temporal** regulada por las siguientes cláusulas: CLAUSULA PRIMERA.- OBJETO. Tal como lo autoriza el numeral 2 del artículo 7o. de la Ley 80 de 1.993, las dos sociedades han concertado participar en la invitación a ofertar, a suscribir y a ejecutar para la Unidad de Planeación Minero-Energética, los servicios especializados de asesoría jurídica antes descrita en forma conjunta y solidaria bajo la modalidad de una unión temporal regulada por el presente documento. CLAUSULA SEGUNDA.- ALCANCE: La Unión temporal que por este documento se establece, cubre, por razón de la materia, todas las

Document 16. Constitution of the Temporary Partnership Martínez Córdoba and Associates to draft the 2001 Mining Code project.

relaciones, eventos, derechos y obligaciones que surjan entre los partícipes y de estos frente a la UPME por causa de la oferta conjunta que han formulado y por el contrato de servicios de asesoría jurídica, así como de su ejecución y liquidación.- CLAUSULA TERCERA.- DURACION: La Unión Temporal entrará en vigencia desde la presente fecha y tendrá la duración necesaria para dar cumplimiento a todas las obligaciones asumidas ante la UPME y ante terceros y que tengan origen en la celebración, ejecución y liquidación del contrato de asesoría jurídica antes mencionado. CLAUSULA CUARTA. DENOMINACION Y REPRESENTACION: La presente unión temporal se denominará Union Temporal Martínez Córdoba & Asociados. Como representante de la misma se designa al doctor Aurelio Martínez Canabal como principal y como representante suplente al doctor José María Córdoba Pérez. Estos representantes tienen su domicilio en la Calle 95 No. 11-51, oficina 404. Esta misma dirección será la de la Unión Temporal. CLAUSULA QUINTA.- PORCENTAJES: En la Unión Temporal las dos firmas participarán en los siguientes porcentajes : Martínez Canabal y Cia S.A. en un 67% y Córdoba Cardona Asociados Ltda. en un 33%, sin perjuicio de la solidaridad de que trata la Cláusula Sexta de este documento.- CLAUSULA SEXTA.- SOLIDARIDAD : Sin consideración a la naturaleza divisible o indivisible de las obligaciones emanadas del Contrato de asesoría jurídica con el UPME, ante esta los partícipes responderán solidaria y mancomunadamente. En consecuencia, la UPME podrá requerir y exigir el cumplimiento total de las mencionadas obligaciones, a su arbitrio, a ambos partícipes o a cualquiera de ellos. CLAUSULA SEPTIMA.- CESION: Los partícipes no podrán cederse entre sí o en favor de terceros su interés en la presente Unión Temporal sin la autorización expresa y previa de la UPME. Si la cesión en favor de terceros fuere parcial y a menos que se acuerde otra cosa, cedente y cesionario serán solidariamente responsables ante el otro participante. En ningún caso o evento que pudiere generar responsabilidad entre los partícipes o frente a terceros, habrá lugar a reclamo, cobro o repetición contra la UPME.- CLAUSULA

Document 17. Constitution of the Temporary Partnership Martínez Córdoba and Associates to draft the 2001 Mining Code project, p.2.

documento se suscribe en Santa Fe de Bogotá, a los quince (15) días del mes de enero de mil novecientos noventa y nueve (1.999).

MARTINEZ CANABAL & CIA. S.A.   CORDOBA CARDONA ASOCIADOS LTDA.

ADRIANA MARTINEZ VILLEGAS   JOSE MARIA CORDOBA PEREZ

Document 18. Constitution of the Temporary Partnership Martínez Córdoba and Associates to draft the 2001 Mining Code project, p.3.

REPUBLICA DE COLOMBIA
MINISTERIO DE MINAS Y ENERGIA
UNIDAD DE PLANEACION MINERO-ENERGETICA

Santafé de Bogotá, D.C.,   0 1 FEB. 1999   ·1 ö

Señores
JOSÉ MARÍA CÓRDOBA PÉREZ
AURELIO MARTÍNEZ CANABAL
Martínez y Córdoba, Asociados
Santafé de Bogotá D.C.

Apreciados señores:

Como es de su conocimiento el Gobierno Nacional y en particular el Ministerio de
Minas y Energía, a través de su Viceministra de Minas, la Doctora Luisa Fernanda
Lafaurie y de esta UNIDAD, han definido como una de sus prioridades la preparación,
trámite y aprobación de una legislación minera acorde con las nuevas realidades del
desarrollo colombiano y a las tendencias modernas del desarrollo minero.

En razón de lo anterior y dada la especialidad del soporte requerido y la urgencia para
disponer de un Código de Minas adoptado e implementado, hemos considerado solicitar a
ustedes propuesta técnica y económica para el propósito, de acuerdo con los Términos de
Referencia Generales adjuntos y con las especificaciones que en él se detallan, esperando
nos sea enviada con la mayor brevedad posible.

Cordial saludo,

ANGELA INÉS CADENA MONROY
Directora General

Copia: Doctora Luisa Fernanda Lafaurie, Viceministra de Minas

AHR/ECL

Avenida 40A No. 13-09-Piso 5, Edificio UGI, Santafé de Bogotá D.C., Colombia.
☎ 3383050 -3203288 -FAX: 2887419 - 2874125
e-mail: upme@upme.gov.co   http://www.upme.gov.co

Document 19. Request by UPME for technical and economic proposals
from the Temporary Partnership Martínez Córdoba and associates to draft
the mining code.

```
"01"           ■202294б8■
```

CAMARA DE COMERCIO DE BOGOTA

SEDE CENTRO

01 DE JUNIO DEL 2001   HORA 08:11:42

01TS1060100100RXK0822   HOJA : 001

* *

CERTIFICADO DE EXISTENCIA Y REPRESENTACION LEGAL O INSCRIPCION DE DOCUMENTOS.
LA CAMARA DE COMERCIO DE BOGOTA, CON FUNDAMENTO EN LAS MATRICULAS E INSCRIPCIONES DEL REGISTRO MERCANTIL,

CERTIFICA :

NOMBRE   :   LADRILLERA   SANTA FE S.A PUDIENDO UTILIZAR LAS DENOMINACIONES SANTAFE Y SANT
N.I.T. : 08600007624
DOMICILIO : BOGOTA D.C.

CERTIFICA :

MATRICULA NO. 00009322

CERTIFICA :

CONSTITUCION: ESCRITURA PUBLICA NO.2.790, NOTARIA 4A. BOGOTA, EL 30 DE MAYO DE 1.955, INSCRITA EL 7 DE JUNIO DE 1.955, BAJO EL NO.31.915 DEL LIBRO RESPECTIVO, SE CONSTITUYO LA SOCIEDAD DENO-MINADA "LADRILLERA SANTA FE LIMITADA."

CERTIFICA :

QUE POR E.P. NO.1464 NOTARIA 45 DE SANTAFE DE BOGOTA DEL 10 DE MA YO DE 1.993, INSCRITA LOS DIAS 18 DE JUNIO DE 1.993 Y 21 DE SEP-TIEMBRE DE 1.994 BAJO LOS NOS. 409.738 Y 463.636 DEL LIBRO IX, LA SOCIEDAD CAMBIO SU NOMBRE DE: LADRILLERA SANTA FE S.A., POR EL DE LADRILLERA SANTAFE S.A. PUDIENDO UTILIZAR LAS DENOMINACIONES SANTAFE Y SANTAFE S.A. INDISTINTAMENTE.-

CERTIFICA :

QUE POR ESCRITURA PUBLICA NO.1.456 OTORGADA EN LA NOTARIA 4A. DE BOGOTA EL 2 DE ABRIL DE 1.968, INSCRITA EN ESTA CAMARA DE COMER-CIO EL 17 DE ABRIL DE 1.968, BAJO EL NO.38.700 DEL LIBRO RESPEC-TIVO LA SOCIEDAD SE TRANSFORMO DE LIMITADA EN SOCIEDAD ANONIMA BAJO EL NOMBRE DE "LADRILLERA SANTA FE S.A."

CERTIFICA :

REFORMAS:

ESCRITURAS NO.	FECHA	NOTARIA	INSCRIPCION
2.267	23-VIII-1957	6A. BOGOTA	28-VIII-1957-37946
7.365	13-XII-1957	4A. BOGOTA	19-XII-1957-38839
3.613	15-VI-1960	5A. BOGOTA	22-VI-1960-46757
2.013	23-IV-1961	4A. BOGOTA	6-V-1961-49675
6.097	16-XI-1961	4A. BOGOTA	27-XI-1961-51758
2.342	12-V-1962	4A. BOGOTA	28-V-1962-53685
1.770	29-IV-1963	4A. BOGOTA	9-V-1963-57000
3.958	27-VIII-1963	4A. BOGOTA	2-IX-1963-58223
757	24-II-1964	4A. BOGOTA	3-III-1964-60142
1.641	13-IV-1965	4A. BOGOTA	22-IV-1965-64063
5.818	22-XII-1966	4A. BOGOTA	14-I-1967 - 70935
757	23-II-1968	4A. BOGOTA	6-III-1968 -75423
107	20-X-1970	11 BOGOTA	22-X-197- 43123
1.957	28-XI-1972	11. BOGOTA	13-XII-1972 - 6479

Document 20. Certificate of existense and legal representation of Ladrilla Santafé, belonging to family of former Colombian President Pastrana Arango.

2.754	5-XII-1974	11. BOGOTA	3-III-1975- 25002
4.466	31-VIII-1977	6. BOGOTA	29-IX-1977 - 50165
208	21-II-1979	11- BOGOTA	21-III-1979 -68774
990	13-VII-1979	11. BOGOTA	21-VIII-1979-73876
1.503	16 XII-1982	28. BOGOTA	7-VI- 1983NO.134100
1.787	23-VIII-1983	32. BOGOTA	23-VIII-1983 NO.137756
2.212	29-VII -1987	32. BOGOTA	31-VII -1987 NO.216173
2.738	24-VII -1989	32. BOGOTA	9-VIII -1989 NO.271804
1.207	24-VI -1991	45. BOGOTA	3-VII -1991 NO.331265
2.465	15-XI -1991	45 STAFE.BTA.	3-XII -1991 NO.347708
1.464	10-V -1993	45 STAFE.BTA. 18-VI	-1993 NO.409738
1.464	10-V -1993	45 STAFE.BTA. 21-IX	-1994 NO.463636
0001547 1998/05/06	00045 SANTA FE DE BOG		00635149 1998/05/22
0002571 1998/07/30	00045 SANTA FE DE BOG		00644798 1998/08/11
0005128 1998/10/14	00042 SANTA FE DE BOG		00653288 1998/10/16
0001461 1998/12/18	00043 SANTA FE DE BOG		00661398 1998/12/18

CERTIFICA :

VIGENCIA: QUE LA SOCIEDAD NO SE HALLA DISUELTA. DURACION HASTA EL 31 DE DICIEMBRE DEL 2020 .

CERTIFICA :

OBJETO SOCIAL: LA SOCIEDAD TENDRA POR OBJETO PRINCIPAL EL DESARROLLO DE LAS SIGUIENTES ACTIVIDADES: 1) LA FABRICACION, TRANSFORMACION, PROCESAMIENTO, ADQUISICION Y/ O ENAJENACION DE LADRILLOS O CUALQUIER OTRO ELEMENTO SEMEJANTE QUE SIRVA PARA LA INDUSTRIA DE LA CONSTRUCCION. 2) LA ADQUISICION, ENAJENACION, EXPLORACION, EXTRACCION, TRANSFORMACION, BENEFICIO, Y / O EXPLOTACION DE MINERALES U OTRAS MATERIAS PRIMAS, PRODUCTOS BASICOS Y/O SEMIELABORACION Y DEMAS ELEMENTOS PROPIOS PARA LA INDUSTRIA LADRILLERA. 3) LA ADQUISICION, ENAJENACION, TRANSFORMACION, PROCESAMIENTO Y/O FABRICACION DE OTROS MATERIALES O ACCESORIOS DESTINADOS A LA CONSTRUCCION, PUDIENDO ADEMAS REPRESENTAR O AGENCIAR FABRICAS, COMP A| IAS COMERCIALIZADORAS, NACIONALES O EXTRANJERAS, QUE SE DEDIQUEN A LA EXTRACCION, FABRICACION, PRODUCCION TRANSFORMACION, VENTA Y/O DISTRIBUCION DE MATERIALES, MAQUINARIAS O EQUIPOS DESTINADOS A LA CONSTRUCCION DE MINERIA. 4) ADMINISTRAR, PROMOVER Y EXPLOTAR LA INDUSTRIA DE LA CONSTRUCCION EN FORMA DIRECTA O MEDIANTE SUBCONTRATACION. EN DESARROLLO DEL OBJETO ANTES ENUNCIADO, LA SOCIEDAD PODRA PROMOVER Y FUNDAR ESTABLECIMIENTOS, ALMACENES, DEPOSITOS O AGENCIAS; PODRA ADEMAS ADQUIRIR A CUALQUIER TITULO TODA CLASE DE BIENES MUEBLES O INMUEBLES, ARRENDARLOS, ENAJENARLOS O GRAVARLOS Y DARLOS EN GARANTIA DE SUS PROPIAS OBLIGACIONES; ADQUIRIR TODA CLASE DE DERECHOS MINEROS, PERMISOS O LICENCIAS, EJECUTAR ASOCIACIONES, APORTE Y/ O CONCESIONES PARA EXPLORAR Y EXPLOTAR MINAS O YACIMIENTOS; EXPLOTAR MARCAS, NOMBRES COMERCIALES, PATENTES INVENCIONES O CUALQUIER OTRO BIEN INCORPORAL, SIEMPRE QUE SEAN AFINES CON EL OBJETO PRINCIPAL, GIRAR, ACEPTAR, ENDOSAR, COBRAR Y PAGAR TODA CLASE DE TITULOS VALORES. CELEBRAR CONTRATOS DE MUTUO, SEGURO, TRANSPORTE, CUENTAS EN PARTICIPACION, PARTICIPAR EN LICITACIONES, CELEBRAR CONTRATOS CON ENTIDADES BANCARIAS O FINANCIERAS Y EN FIN REALIZAR TODA CLASE DE OPERACIONES CON TITULOS VALORES. PODRA ADQUIRIR ACCIONES, CUOTAS O PARTES DE INTERES EN OTRAS SOCIEDADES, O FORMAR PARTE DE CORPORACIONES, ASOCIACIONES O SOCIEDADES ORDINARIAS DE MINAS, QUE TENGAN ACTIVIDADES IGUALES, SEMEJANTES O COMPLEMENTARIAS. ADEMAS PODRA REALIZAR O PRESTAR ASESORIAS EN GENERAL Y CELEBRAR TODO ACTO O CONTRATO QUE SE RELACIONE CON EL OBJETO SOCIAL PRINCIPAL. 5·)

Document 21. Certificate of existence and legal representation of Ladrilla Santafé, p.2.

```
*01*              * 2 0 2 2 9 9 6 9 *
          CAMARA DE COMERCIO DE BOGOTA

                    SEDE CENTRO

          01 DE JUNIO DEL 2001           HORA 08:11:43

          01TS1060100100RXK0822            HOJA : 002

          * * * * * * * * * * * * * * * * * * * * * *
```

HACER APORTES DE CAPITAL, ADQUIRIR ACCIONES O PARTICIPACIONES Y
EN GENERAL INVERTIR EN SOCIEDADES Y CONTRATOS EN CUENTAS EN
PARTICIPACION, DE CUALQUIER ESPECIE, EN EL PAIS O EN EL EXTERIOR.
                         CERTIFICA :
CAPITAL:
                    ** CAPITAL AUTORIZADO **
VALOR   :$21,999,999,960.00000
NO. DE ACCIONES:122,222,222.00
VALOR NOMINAL :$180.00000
                    ** CAPITAL SUSCRITO **
VALOR   :$21,556,237,680.00000
NO. DE ACCIONES:119,756,876.00
VALOR NOMINAL :$180.00000
                    ** CAPITAL PAGADO **
VALOR   :$21,556,237,680.00000
NO. DE ACCIONES:119,756,876.00
VALOR NOMINAL :$180.00000
                       CERTIFICA :
              ** JUNTA DIRECTIVA: PRINCIPAL(ES) **
QUE POR ACTA NO. 0000037 DE ASAMBLEA DE ACCIONISTAS DEL 18 DE
DICIEMBRE DE 1998   INSCRITA EL 18 DE DICIEMBRE DE 1998 BAJO EL
NUMERO 00661399 DEL LIBRO IX , FUE(RON) NOMBRADO(S):
       NOMBRE   IDENTIFICACION
PRIMER RENGLON
  URIBE CRANE ANDRES   C.C.00002854438
SEGUNDO RENGLON
  URIBE ARANGO CARLOS ANDRES   C.C.00079149905
QUE POR ACTA NO. 0000040 DE ASAMBLEA DE ACCIONISTAS DEL 15 DE
AGOSTO DEL 2000 , INSCRITA EL 22 DE AGOSTO DEL 2000 BAJO EL
NUMERO 00741655 DEL LIBRO IX , FUE(RON) NOMBRADO(S):
       NOMBRE   IDENTIFICACION
TERCER RENGLON
  URIBE ARANGO RICARDO   C.C.00079937642
QUE POR ACTA NO. 0000037 DE ASAMBLEA DE ACCIONISTAS DEL 18 DE
DICIEMBRE DE 1998 , INSCRITA EL 18 DE DICIEMBRE DE 1998 BAJO EL
NUMERO 00661399 DEL LIBRO IX , FUE(RON) NOMBRADO(S):
       NOMBRE   IDENTIFICACION
CUARTO RENGLON
  URRUTIA VALENZUELA CARLOS   C.C.00019088535
QUINTO RENGLON
  LONDO#O JARAMILLO HERNANDO   C.C.00002898813
              ** JUNTA DIRECTIVA: SUPLENTE(S) **
QUE POR ACTA NO. 0000040 DE ASAMBLEA DE ACCIONISTAS DEL 15 DE
AGOSTO DEL 2000 , INSCRITA EL 22 DE AGOSTO DEL 2000 BAJO EL
NUMERO 00741655 DEL LIBRO IX , FUE(RON) NOMBRADO(S):
       NOMBRE   IDENTIFICACION
```

Document 22. Certificate of existence and legal representation of Ladrillera Santafé, p.3.
```

~~PRIMER RENGLON~~
    VILLA DE VAN COTHEM LAURA   C.C.00020298815
QUE POR ACTA NO. 0000037 DE ASAMBLEA DE ACCIONISTAS DEL 18 DE
DICIEMBRE DE 1998 , INSCRITA EL 18 DE DICIEMBRE DE 1998 BAJO EL
NUMERO 00661399 DEL LIBRO IX , FUE(RON) NOMBRADO(S):
        NOMBRE   IDENTIFICACION
SEGUNDO RENGLON
    PEREA GOMEZ ENRIQUE   C.C.00019090845
QUE POR ACTA NO. 0000040 DE ASAMBLEA DE ACCIONISTAS DEL 15 DE
AGOSTO DEL 2000 , INSCRITA EL 22 DE AGOSTO DEL 2000 BAJO EL
NUMERO 00741655 DEL LIBRO IX , FUE(RON) NOMBRADO(S):
        NOMBRE   IDENTIFICACION
TERCER RENGLON
    RESTREPO GOMEZ LUIS FELIPE RUPERTO   C.C.00079151174
QUE POR ACTA NO. 0000037 DE ASAMBLEA DE ACCIONISTAS DEL 18 DE
DICIEMBRE DE 1998 , INSCRITA EL 18 DE DICIEMBRE DE 1998 BAJO EL
NUMERO 00661399 DEL LIBRO IX , FUE(RON) NOMBRADO(S):
        NOMBRE   IDENTIFICACION
CUARTO RENGLON
    ZULETA MARIA MARGARITA   C.C.00039692854
QUINTO RENGLON
    ZARATE DIAZ GRANADOS NANCY MILENA INES DEL C.C.00039686259
    SOCORRO
                        CERTIFICA :
REPRESENTACION LEGAL: EL REPRESENTANTE LEGAL ES EL PRESIDENTE,
QUIEN TENDRA DOS (2) SUPLENTES, PRIMERO Y SEGUNDO, QUIENES LO
REEMPLAZARAN EN SUS FALTAS ABSOLUTAS, TEMPORALES O ACCIDENTALES.
                        CERTIFICA :
                 ** NOMBRAMIENTOS : **
QUE POR ACTA NO. 0000338 DE JUNTA DIRECTIVA DEL 22 DE DICIEMBRE
DE 1998 , INSCRITA EL 23 DE DICIEMBRE DE 1998 BAJO EL NUMERO
00661934 DEL LIBRO IX , FUE(RON) NOMBRADO(S):
        NOMBRE   IDENTIFICACION
PRESIDENTE
    ECHAVARRIA BUSTAMANTE JAIRO ANTONIO   C.C.00008301638
QUE POR ACTA NO. 0000345 DE JUNTA DIRECTIVA DEL 20 DE OCTUBRE DE
1999 , INSCRITA EL 29 DE DICIEMBRE DE 1999 BAJO EL NUMERO
00710207 DEL LIBRO IX , FUE(RON) NOMBRADO(S):
        NOMBRE   IDENTIFICACION
PRIMER SUPLENTE DEL PRESIDENTE
    PEREA GOMEZ ENRIQUE   C.C.00019090845
SEGUNDO SUPLENTE DEL PRESIDENTE
    ZARATE DIAZ GRANADOS NANCY MILENA INES DEL C.C.00039686259
    SOCORRO
                        CERTIFICA :
FACULTADES DEL REPRESENTANTE LEGAL: EL PRESIDENTE EJERCERA LAS
FUNCIONES DE SU CARGO Y EN ESPECIAL LAS SIGUIENTES: 1. PLANEAR EN
EL CORTO Y LARGO PLAZO LAS ACTIVIDADES SOCIALES EN COORDINACION
CON LA JUNTA DIRECTIVA DE LA SOCIEDAD. 2. REPRESENTAR A LA
SOCIEDAD JUDICIAL Y EXTRAJUDICIALMENTE, ANTE LOS ASOCIADOS, ANTE
TERCEROS Y ANTE TODA CLASE DE AUTORIDADES JUDICIALES Y
ADMINISTRATIVAS; 3. EJECUTAR LOS ACUERDOS Y RESOLUCIONES DE LA
ASAMBLEAS (SIC) GENERAL Y DE LA JUNTA DIRECTIVA. 4. REALIZAR Y
CELEBRAR LOS ACTOS O CONTRATOS QUE TIENDAN A LLENAR LOS FINES
DE LA SOCIEDAD, SIEMPRE QUE ESTOS NO EXCEDAN LOS LIMITES FIJADOS
EN LA CLAUSULA 47, ORDINAL 16., PUES EN ESTE CASO REQUERIRA LA
AUTORIZACION DE LA JUNTA DIRECTIVA. 5. SOMETER A ARBITRAMENTO O

Document 23. Certificate of existence and legal representation of Ladrillera Santafé, p.4.

CAMARA DE COMERCIO DE BOGOTA

SEDE CENTRO

01 DE JUNIO DEL 2001

HORA 08:11:43

01TS1060100100RXK0822

HOJA : 003

* * * * * * * * * * * * * * * * * * * *

TRANSIGIR LAS DIFERENCIAS DE LA SOCIEDAD CON TERCEROS, CON SUJECION A LAS LIMITACIONES DEL ARTICULO 47, ORDINAL 16. CITADO. 6. PRESENTAR A LA JUNTA DIRECTIVA LOS ESTADOS FINANCIEROS, ADEMAS DE UN BALANCE ANUAL. 7. PRESENTAR EN ASOCIO CON LA JUNTA DIRECTIVA LOS INFORMES Y DOCUMENTOS DE QUE TRATA EL ARTICULO 446 DEL CODIGO DE COMERCIO. 8. NOMBRAR Y REMOVER LOS EMPLEADOS DE LA SOCIEDAD CUYA DESIGNACION O REMOCION NO CORRESPONDA A LA JUNTA DIRECTIVA O A LA ASAMBLEA. 9. DELEGAR DETERMINADAS FUNCIONES PROPIAS DE SU CARGO Y DENTRO DE LOS LIMITES SE#ALADOS EN LOS ESTATUTOS. 10. CUIDAR DE LA RECAUDACION E INVERSION DE LOS FONDOS DE LA EMPRESA. 11. VELAR PORQUE TODOS LOS EMPLEADOS DE LA SOCIEDAD CUMPLAN ESTRICTAMENTE SUS DEBERES Y PONER EN CONOCIMIENTO DE LA ASAMBLEA O DE LA JUNTA DIRECTIVA LAS IRREGULARIDADES O FALTAS GRAVES QUE OCURRAN SOBRE ESTE PARTICULAR. 12. CONFERIR PODERES GENERALES O ESPECIALES PARA LA REPRESENTACION DE LA SOCIEDAD ANTE CUALQUIER AUTORIDAD, Y; 13. CUMPLIR LAS DEMAS FUNCIONES QUE LE CORRESPONDEN POR DISPOSICION DE LA LEY, LOS ESTATUTOS, LA ASAMBLEA GENERAL O LA JUNTA DIRECTIVA. CORRESPONDE A LA JUNTA DIRECTIVA: AUTORIZAR AL PRESIDENTE O A SUS SUPLENTES LA ADQUISICION, ENAJENACION, LIMITACION O GRAVAMEN DE INMUEBLES SIN CONSIDERACION A SU CUANTIA. AUTORIZAR AL REPRESENTANTE LEGAL PARA CELEBRAR CUALQUIER ACTO O CONTRATO QUE EXCEDA LA SUMA EQUIVALENTE EN PESOS A CINCO MIL (5.000) UNIDADES DE PODER ADQUISITIVO CONSTANTE -UPAC- EN LA FECHA DE CELEBRACION DEL ACTO O CONTRATO, SALVO CUANDO SE TRATE DE ENAJENACION DE LADRILLO O CUALQUIER OTRO ELEMENTO SEMEJANTE QUE SIRVA PARA LA INDUSTRIA DE LA CONSTRUCCION O DE LA ADQUISICION DE INSUMOS NECESARIOS PARA LA PRODUCCION O DE LA INVERSION EN TITULOS, EXCEPTUADAS LAS ACCIONES, EMITIDAS POR ENTIDADES PUBLICAS O PRIVADAS SOMETIDAS A VIGILANCIA ESTATAL, PUES EN ESTOS CASOS EL REPRESENTANTE LEGAL PODRA ACTUAR AUTONOMAMENTE Y SIN LIMITACION ALGUNA.

CERTIFICA :

** REVISOR FISCAL: **

QUE POR ACTA NO. 0000033 DE ASAMBLEA DE ACCIONISTAS DEL 14 DE MARZO DE 1996 , INSCRITA EL 10 DE JULIO DE 1996 BAJO EL NUMERO 00545296 DEL LIBRO IX , FUE(RON) NOMBRADO(S):

NOMBRE   IDENTIFICACION
REVISOR FISCAL PRINCIPAL
MORENO TOVAR RODRIGO
                                                   C.C.00000029105

QUE POR ACTA NO. 0000034 DE ASAMBLEA DE ACCIONISTAS DEL 11 DE MARZO DE 1997 , INSCRITA EL 05 DE AGOSTO DE 1997 BAJO EL NUMERO 00596426 DEL LIBRO IX , FUE(RON) NOMBRADO(S):

NOMBRE   IDENTIFICACION
REVISOR FISCAL SUPLENTE
ACOSTA CAMELO ROSAURA
                                                   C.C.00041564378

Document 24. Certificate of existence and legal representation of Ladrillera Santafé, p.5.

CERTIFICA :
PERMISO DE FUNCIONAMIENTO: QUE POR RESOLUCION NO.2836 DEL 8 DE
JUNIO DE 1.968, INSCRITA EL 11 DE JUNIO DE 1.968, BAJO EL NO.
39.019 DEL LIBRO RESPECTIVO, LA SUPERINTENDENCIA DE SOCIEDADES
ANONIMAS OTORGO PERMISO DEFINITIVO DE FUNCIONAMIENTO A ESTA SO-
CIEDAD.
                           CERTIFICA :
DIRECCION DE NOTIFICACION JUDICIAL : CRA 9 NO. 74-08 OFC 602
MUNICIPIO : BOGOTA D.C.
                           CERTIFICA :
QUE POR DOCUMENTO PRIVADO DE SANTA FE DE BOGOTA D.C. DEL 24 DE
FEBRERO DE 1998 , INSCRITO EL 06 DE MARZO DE 1998 BAJO EL NUMERO
00625314 DEL LIBRO IX , SE COMUNICO QUE SE HA CONFIGURADO UNA
SITUACION DE   CONTROL POR PARTE DE LA SOCIEDAD MATRIZ:LADRILLERA
SANTA FE S.A PUDIENDO UTILIZAR LAS DENOMINACIONES SANTAFE Y SANT,
RESPECTO DE LAS SIGUIENTES SOCIEDADES SUBORDINADAS:
- MINERA DE LOS ANDES S.A.
DOMICILIO : SANTA FE DE BOGOTA D.C.
- COMPA#IA MINERA LTDA
DOMICILIO : SANTA FE DE BOGOTA D.C.
- LOSAS LTDA
DOMICILIO : SANTA FE DE BOGOTA D.C.
QUE POR DOCUMENTO PRIVADO DE SANTA FE DE BOGOTA D.C. DEL 18 DE
DICIEMBRE DE 1998 , INSCRITO EL 01 DE DICIEMBRE DE 1999 BAJO EL
NUMERO 00706024 DEL LIBRO IX , SE COMUNICO QUE SE HA CONFIGURADO
UNA SITUACION DE GRUPO EMPRESARIAL POR PARTE DE LA SOCIEDAD
MATRIZ:LADRILLERA   SANTA   FE   S.A   PUDIENDO UTILIZAR LAS
DENOMINACIONES   SANTAFE Y SANT, RESPECTO DE LAS SIGUIENTES
SOCIEDADES SUBORDINADAS:
- SANTAFE TILE CORPORATION
DOMICILIO : (FUERA DEL PAIS)
                           CERTIFICA :
QUE NO FIGURAN INSCRIPCIONES ANTERIORES A LA FECHA DEL PRESENTE
CERTIFICADO, QUE MODIFIQUEN TOTAL O PARCIALMENTE SU CONTENIDO.

DE CONFORMIDAD CON LO CONCEPTUADO POR LA SUPERINTENDENCIA DE
INDUSTRIA Y COMERCIO, LOS ACTOS DE REGISTRO AQUI CERTIFICADOS
QUEDAN EN FIRME CINCO (5) DIAS HABILES DESPUES DE LA FECHA DE
PUBLICACION EN EL BOLETIN DEL REGISTRO DE LA CORRESPONDIENTE
INSCRIPCION, SIEMPRE QUE NO SEAN OBJETO DE RECURSOS EN LA VIA
GUBERNATIVA.

EL SECRETARIO DE LA CAMARA DE COMERCIO,

VALOR : $ 2,000.00

DE CONFORMIDAD CON EL DECRETO 2150 DE 1995 Y LA AUTORIZACION
IMPARTIDA POR LA SUPERINTENDENCIA DE INDUSTRIA Y COMERCIO,
MEDIANTE EL OFICIO DEL 18 DE NOVIEMBRE DE 1996, LA FIRMA MECANICA
QUE APARECE A CONTINUACION TIENE PLENA VALIDEZ PARA TODOS LOS
EFECTOS LEGALES.

Document 25. Certificate of existence and legal representation of Ladrillera Santafé, p.6.

About the Author and Translator

Francisco Ramírez Cuellar is a Colombian lawyer, unionist, and human rights activist. He is president of Sintraminercol, the Colombian mining workers union, and Human Rights Secretary of Funtraenergética, the Colombian federation of energy-sector unions. His union has taken a leading role in the struggle against the privatization of Colombia's mineral resources, in exposing the abuses of multinational corporations in the mining and energy sector, and in pressing for legislative reform to return some of the profits of the mining sector to the country. The union has been active in the defense of the rights of indigenous and Afro-Colombian people displaced by mining and energy projects and in environmental issues, as well as labor issues. The Spanish version of his book, *La gran mineria en Colombia: las ganancias del exterminio*, was published in Colombia in 2004.

Aviva Chomsky is professor of Latin American History and coordinator of Latin American, Latino and Caribbean Studies at Salem State College in Massachusetts. Her books include *West Indian Workers and the United Fruit Company in Costa Rica, 1870-1940* (Louisiana State University Press, 1996); *Identity and Struggle at the Margins of the Nation-State: The Laboring Peoples of Central America and the Hispanic Caribbean* (co-edited with Aldo Lauria-Santiago, Duke University Press 1998) and *The Cuba Reader: History, Culture, Politics* (co-edited with Barry Carr and Pamela Smorkaloff, Duke University Press, 2003), as well as numerous articles and essays. She has been active in Central America, Cuba, and Colombia solidarity work for over twenty years.